Emotion in Sp〔

Emotion is central to human character, infiltrating our physiological functions and our mental constitution. In sport, athletes feel emotion in specific ways, from joy to anger and despair.

This is the first book to examine emotion in sport from a philosophical perspective, building on concepts developed by ancient Greek and modern philosophers. For instance, how is Aristotle's concept of *catharsis* applied to the sports field? How about *power* as advanced by Nietzsche, or *existentialism* as discussed by Kierkegaard? *Emotion in Sports* explores the philosophical framework for the expression of emotion and relates it to our psychological understanding, from the perspective of both athlete and spectator.

A fascinating and useful read for students, researchers, scholars, and practitioners in the fields of sport sciences, philosophy, and psychology.

Yunus Tuncel teaches Philosophy at The New School, New York, USA and in New York University's Liberal Studies Program. He is a member of the International Association for the Philosophy of Sport (IAPS) and is co-founder of the Nietzsche Circle, serving on its Board of Directors and the Editorial Board of its electronic journal, *The Agonist*. In addition to Nietzsche and history of philosophy, he is interested in 20th-century French thought and recent artistic, philosophical, and cultural movements, including postmodernity and post-humanism. His primary areas of research are art, dance, experiences of the body in general, culture, music, myth, sports, and spectacle. He is interested in the fusion of art, sport, and philosophy in various cultural formations.

Ethics and Sport

Series editors: Mike McNamee
University of Wales Swansea

Jim Parry
University of Leeds

The Ethics and Sport series aims to encourage critical reflection on the practice of sport, and to stimulate professional evaluation and development. Each volume explores new work relating to philosophical ethics and the social and cultural study of ethical issues. Each is different in scope, appeal, focus, and treatment but a balance is sought between local and international focus, perennial, and contemporary issues, level of audience, teaching, and research application, and variety of practical concerns.

Recent titles include:

Bioethics, Genetics, and Sport
Silvia Camporesi and Mike McNamee

Body Ecology and Emersive Leisure
Edited by Bernard Andrieu, Jim Parry, Alessandro Porrovecchio and Olivier Sirost

Sport, Ethics, and Philosophy
Edited by Mike McNamee

Philosophy and Nature Sports
Kevin Krein

Emotion in Sports
Philosophical Perspectives
Yunus Tuncel

For more information about this series, please visit: www.routledge.com/Ethics-and-Sport/book-series/EANDS

Contents

Acknowledgments

I would like to thank Michael McNamee for inspiring and supporting me in this journey. Without him this book would not have been possible. The idea emerged when he heard my talk at the IAPS conference in Cardiff and he asked me to submit a proposal. In addition, many thanks go to many members and supporters of the International Association for the Philosophy of Sport. I have met several wonderful scholars and enjoyed many discussions at its conferences. Many ideas to write essays and to create anthologies emerged from these gatherings, some with booze, some without. I should start with David Kilpatrick who introduced me to IAPS and extend my gratitude to Scott Kretchmar, Gunnar Breivik, Jim Parry, Jeffrey Fry, Javi Frias, Jesus Ilundain, Cesar Torres, John Russell, Emanuel Isidori, Ron Welters, Gunnar Breivik, Kenneth Aggerhold, and Charlene Weaving.

When I embarked on this book, I must confess that I was lost in the vast ocean of literature and occasionally fell into despair. Often we forget, but we should remember, that our friends who share our passions encourage us to remain firm and pursue. I cannot thank enough the following people who share the joys and perils of being on a philosophical path: Luke Trusso, Alec Ontiveros, Kaitlyn Creasy, Robert Schaecher, Aysegul Durakoglu, Michael Steinmann, Stefan L. Sorgner, Jaime del Val, Francesca Ferrando, Jared Russell, Rodrigo Ferreira Flores, Sabine Roehr, Jack Fitzgerald, Aaron Simon, and Seth Binsted. I must also add my brother, Emre Tuncel, and my friends Can Bulucu, Beril Bayrak and Cem Aydogan, for their support and for being there for me in moments of despair.

Many thanks go to Rainer J. Hanshe for editing the first draft of my manuscripts, Jared Russell for his feedback, and the editors and reviewers of Routledge, including the three blind reviewers for their thoughtful input. Finally, I thank my parents for their support from far away and my wife, Meltem Paker, and daughter, Mayra Paker Tuncel, for harboring a heterogenous rebel cloaked as a homogeneous conformist.

Introduction

When I wrote my first paper on emotions in sport and presented it at the IAPS conference in Cardiff in 2014, I had no idea that I would eventually write a book on the same topic. For that I am thankful to Michael McNamee and Routledge. I cannot forget those few days I spent in Cardiff, nor the hospitality of the locals. After much research and reflection, I asked myself how I got entangled in this immense topic and how I would emerge from it with some success; after all, one could write one book on this topic for and according to every single school of philosophy. My readers will be the judges of the outcome. Before I could make any claims on emotion in sport, the first challenge I faced was developing an understanding of emotion itself. I had to provide a preliminary understanding of emotion and all the related phenomena.

Emotion is a crucial dimension of human existence, a dimension still not sufficiently understood; scholars and psychologists are trying to understand it based on speculation, experience, and research. Emotions are experienced throughout our entire being, from body to soul, mind, and language. Emotions are affected by physiological conditions that have to do with our unique bodies, psychic conditions that often remain unconscious, and cognitive conditions, too. Finally, in addition to gesturally, we express emotions linguistically. Any approach that does not consider the human being as integral (mind-body-soul) is incomplete in part. For some time, philosophers dismissed emotions, each in their own different way, and placed them under the rule of the mind; the Stoics took a radical approach and believed emotions could be controlled by the mind. This position leaves us only to be immature in relation to our emotional composition, which I believe is the case with humanity at this stage of its evolution, as we are all configurations of repressed emotions. While some emotions can be controlled by the mind, in general they cannot, not to speak of the diversity of emotions and their different nature. They have their own integral developments and dimensions that cannot be understood or transformed solely through cognitive intervention. In most cases, the mental control of emotions is simply the avoidance of emotion and the refusal to address emotional 'problems.'

Contrary to Stoicism, William James emphasizes the physiological aspect of emotion (James 1884). For James, our emotional life is caught up in our bodily frame and our feelings are the fruits of the same soil with the grossest bodily sensations of pleasure and pain (25). While the role that physiological functions play in our emotional make-up cannot be dismissed, it comprises only one dimension of our emotional composition. The same person can have different emotional responses to the same physiological condition depending upon various factors (one's general emotional or physical state, etc.); the variety of such emotional responses already refutes entirely James' theory and shows its limitation. Take, for instance, a man who has a low tolerance for hunger and becomes cranky and angry at the first hunger pang. If such a man goes through a practice of fasting and grows accustomed to hunger to some extent, he will most likely not have the same emotional response at the first pang of hunger.

As Darwin distinguishes when using the idea of universality (1872/1998), emotions can be deep or superficial, basic, and non-basic (basic and derivative). What these basic emotions are have been a point of disagreement among philosophers: for the Stoics,[1] they include delight, distress, desire, and fear (Graver 2007); Epicurus finds pain and pleasure (and their related feelings) to be foundational and builds his theory upon them. Whereas other philosophers speak of emotion, feeling or affect, Hobbes refers to them instead as passions and proposes seven passions: appetite, desire, love, aversion, hatred, joy, and grief (1668/1994). Finally, Descartes' list includes admiration-surprise, love, hate, desire, joy, and sadness (1649/1989: Part 2), while for Spinoza there are three fundamental emotions (1989: 177): desire, pleasure, and displeasure or pain (although his full list of all emotions includes close to 50 emotions). Given cultural and individual differences, devising such lists is highly tentative; however, to claim that there are primordial emotions seated in the deeper strata of human existence is not a far-fetched idea.

Related to the physiological model, and even to Darwin's theory, is the projectivist theory, examined critically by Johnston, which claims that human beings generate certain emotions (especially the basic ones) so that they can preserve their lives and keep a distance from what may infect or kill them (2001: 185–186). For instance, we may be disgusted by carcasses or rotten food, feces, or some seemingly dangerous animals; even if the disgust is not in these objects per se, we experience the emotion of disgust before them as a protective force. Think of fear and the role it plays in preserving human life. However, much of this has subjective variety. While there are human beings who are afraid of the smallest harmless insects and birds, their fear is true to them, but not necessary to preserve their physical lives.[2] This however, could suggest that there is an emotional impact and that such people are protecting their emotional well-being.

Emotions can be reflections of disposition or object-driven. For instance, a human being who has a low tolerance for hunger may easily be cranky and angry at the first pang of hunger. No object, internal or external, is yet the target of his anger. On the other hand, emotions can take on objects and be internal or external. If a sad thought comes to my mind, I may become sad and start crying; or, if I see a human being in a state of intense suffering and relate to it, I may become sad.

Language cannot be an entirely adequate expression of emotion; language can, in no way, be adequate for anything. Yes, it is a form of expression, but it has limits. Regarding language and its relationship to emotion, the following can be said. First, language may not be able to cover the entire scope of human emotions. Second, language may not be able to reflect the intensity of human emotions. If different words enable us to convey such intensity, there are different scales of intensity, too. In English, for instance, we have dislike, hate, disgust, and odium to express our distance to and repulsion for an object, but there may be some repulsion beyond odium. In short, not every scale of a particular emotion can have a name (no doubt, there are other, non-linguistic, forms of expressing emotions). Finally, there are compound feelings for which there may be no specific linguistic expression; such feelings may be referred to as 'sentiment' or 'mood.' The fact that English has many words to stand for 'emotion' and related phenomena shows the complexity of the subject. I do not intend to convolute the semantic field here, but the words 'emotion,' 'feeling,' 'sentiment,' 'passion,' 'mood,' and 'affect' (from Spinoza) have close affinities and reflect different facades of the same human phenomenon, not to mention their different etymologies. Tentatively, I agree with the following definition Goldie offers, which will be examined throughout this book:

> An emotion . . . is a relatively complex state, involving past and present episodes of thoughts, feelings, and bodily changes, dynamically related in a narrative of part of a person's life, together with dispositions to experience further emotional episodes, and to act out of the emotion and to express that emotion. Your expression of emotion and the actions which spring from the emotion, whilst not part of the emotion itself, are none the less part of the narrative which runs through – and beyond – the emotion, mutually affecting and resonating in that emotion, and in further emotions, moods, and traits, and in further actions.
>
> (Goldie 2003: 5)

As for the structure of this book, it has three parts. The first part, 'Theoretical Framework,' is designed to present a theoretical framework for emotions in sport. I do not attempt to present a unique theory of emotion here; instead, I use existing philosophical ideas to draw parameters within which I can examine sport-specific emotions. These include catharsis, affect, power, and quality. Moreover, I benefited from many different disciplines, schools of philosophy, and traditions, but could not have included every school in my discussion due to the specific focus of this work. The second part, 'Sport-Specific Emotions,' discusses emotions as they appear in the context of sport such as joy, fear, anxiety, anger, guilt, sadness, etc. In the third part, 'Care of Emotions,' I examine ideas, methods, and therapeutic interventions to address emotional problems in sports.

The book does not offer a theory of emotion, but rather builds an integral approach and applies it to the sporting context. If the spirit of sport sustains itself in a balance of emotions, what are those emotions? What type of emotional/affective response could upset and ruin the spirit of sport? What are some pathways that can help us deal with emotional problems, as they shed light on analyzing and diagnosing such problems? What follows below is a summary of each chapter.

Part I: theoretical framework

Chapter I: catharsis of emotions

The subject of the discharge of emotions has been at the center of many debates and incorporated into psychological discourse and practice. Although Aristotle developed his theory of catharsis on theater, it has been applied to other areas of human existence and can also be applied to the field of sport. What type of a channel is sport when it comes to expressing our emotions, whether as players or as spectators? In what ways does and can sport serve as a means of dealing with our emotions? This question becomes crucial, especially when we keep in mind the quality of human emotions, the subject matter of Chapter 4 of this book. There is a range of human emotions from low to high, which every human being harbors; to be able to work on the quality of our emotions, if that is established as a goal, we need to express or discharge them – this is where catharsis becomes important. Therefore, its appropriation by psychology is not accidental.

Chapter 2: the question of affect-impact and collective dimension of emotions

Every being produces multiple *affects* and we are connected through these sometimes known, sometimes unknown, affects, rather than a strictly knowable chain of causality. Spinoza introduces this concept and includes emotions within his theory, or what he calls 'passion,' among which he counts joy, sadness, and desire. All beings are somehow linked to each other through a network of *affects*. The things we do and say have an effect on others, which work in their own contexts. Affects can be understood in terms of their intensity, scope, type, etc. In the sporting field, the things athletes do and say have their own affects. When the athletes' fame and the scope of their game increases, the affect often increases accordingly. Affects do not follow any strict chain of causality, but they do shape their immediate environment in ways that are beyond the control of the affect-producing agent. Both the individual and collective dimension of emotions in sport will be discussed in this chapter.

Chapter 3: the feeling of power and power relations

'The feeling of power' may sound strange in English, but it is a direct translation of the German phrase, *Machtsgefühl*, as it appears in Friedrich Nietzsche's works. Nietzsche is the first philosopher to develop a philosophy of power, which is insightful, although it is scattered throughout his writings and has led to many controversial interpretations. The basic claim of this philosophy of power is as follows: we are always in power relations; we exert power on each other in different ways, and there are different forms, or *Gestalts*, of power. Philosophers like Gilles Deleuze and Michel Foucault expanded on Nietzsche's philosophy of power and presented their works in institutional contexts. In this chapter, I will explore power relations in sports and the way the feeling of power manifests itself in the field of sports. For example, how does a victorious team or athlete relate to the defeated one? Or, how do managers and trainers relate to their own players? Or, how do umpires and referees relate to competing athletes? I do not suggest that power relations are only vertical, as is the case in the examples listed here. I plan to explore all vertical and lateral power relations in sport.

Chapter 4: quality of sentiments

In his argument against the priority of reason in matters of morality, David Hume states that sentiments come first and reason is simply a handmaid to them. He then presents a list of sentiments such as benevolence, which, associated with likes and dislikes or attractions and repulsions, lie at the root of our moral actions. Agreeing with Hume but taking his argument further, we can speak of the quality of emotions, of emotions that are both high and low. Clearly, such an assumption will be based on value judgments and not everyone will agree on such determinations. However, it can be argued that there are emotions the expressions of which can be detrimental to the spirit of sporting and its practice either in the short or long run. For instance, excessive outbursts of anger, blaming one's teammates, arrogance in victory, fear of performance (wrongly called "performance anxiety"), or excessive fear in general can be considered low feelings. Inversely, we can speak of uplifting, high-quality emotions that spur sporting practice to higher levels of performance.

Part II: sport-specific emotions (SSE)

Chapter 5: fear, anxiety, pain, suffering, and the question of authenticity

All human beings are faced with the dilemma of who they are and what they can be, whether they recognize it or not; which is to say, what they can be as higher, elevated beings. Different philosophers have spoken of this differently, and the question of transcendence has been understood in different ways in different historic contexts. In our age, transcendence has been this-worldly; we find our 'authenticity,' to use Heidegger's phrase, in our worldly activities; we can transcend ourselves so that we can be authentic, so that we can be who we truly are. Sport is one outlet for such worldly transcendence. In order to achieve such transcendence, we need to overcome our fears and experience anxiety so as to be authentic. Kierkegaard is the first so-called existentialist thinker who presents an interesting picture of 'authenticity' in relation to such basic emotions as fear and anxiety. I will discuss existentialist literature to show how the field of sports is, or can be, such an outlet for becoming authentic, or to use a common phrase, to reach nirvana.

Chapter 6: other specific feelings in sporting context: anger, depression (or despair), envy, guilt, sadness et al.

The previous chapter focused on two special feelings, fear, and anxiety, as they manifest themselves in sport, but what about other sport-related feelings? It will take another whole book to discuss the variety of human emotions that are felt and expressed in the sporting community. Therefore, I took a sample of what I thought was more common. Here is the short list: anger, arrogance-hubris, depression, despair, envy, euphoria, fear, guilt, joy, pain-suffering, pleasure, pride, *Schadenfreude*, shame, and sadness. I will specifically address sport-specific versions of these feelings such as arrogance in victory, play-fear or play-anxiety (analogous to performance anxiety), mass-euphoria in victory, defeat despair, foul shame or foul guilt, teammate anger, prize envy, and so on.

Chapter 7: other specific feelings in sporting contexts: ambition, euphoria, hubris, pride et al.

This chapter is reserved for upbeat emotions in sport, emotions that motivate us, that propel us to strive and excel, such as ambition, without which contest would not exist. Such strife and its outcome produce other high emotions such as joy, pride, and euphoria. However, excessive doses of such emotions can also be detrimental to the spirit of contest and sport and ruinous for us and others, in the short and long run. In this chapter, I examine the dangers of the excess of these emotions and suggest possible antidotes.

Part III: care of emotions

Chapter 8: 'sentimental education' of athletes

Do athletes need to be educated in the way they express their feelings? The question is a deeper one and pertains to the emotional make-up of each individual athlete. As I argue in previous chapters, we can speak of the quality of emotions and the affects of emotions. Athletes come from diverse emotional backgrounds and can, and often do, have, and express very raw, uncultivated emotions. These emotions could be worked on during training with the help of coaches and sport psychologists. If we care so much for the physical being of the athlete, why not for their psychological and emotional well-being? Cesar Torres called it 'sentimental education' in our discussion at the 2015 IAPS conference in Cardiff. Although the term originates from a literary context (Flaubert's 19th-century novel), it can be applied to sports as well. How such an education can be implemented is a practical affair. Philosophers can start the conversation and if our ideas are sound, they will be implemented.

Chapter 9: therapeutic treatment of emotions in sporting practice

I do not suggest that the primary goal of each sport is to educate athletes and make them better human beings; however, sport can become, and often is, an outlet for the externalization of specific feelings, which would normally, i.e. in the absence of sports, lay dormant. For instance, emotions of performance anxiety, despair while losing, euphoria of goal-scoring, joy in victory, joy of playing with and playing against, anger at teammates' poor performance, and guilt after defeat are such emotions; they are sport-specific – needless to say, most if not all of these emotions are not strictly limited to sport and have corollaries in other fields. We have to externalize and express our emotions, whatever they may be, so that we can work on and better understand them. Sport training and practice can be arenas for a therapeutics of emotions, therapeutics as understood in the broad sense of the original Greek word as healing. Sport heals in many ways, but the focus here is on emotional healing.

Chapter 10: emotion vs. action: physiological, psychological, linguistic, and rational aspects of emotion

What comes first? Emotion or action? Do we feel a specific emotion because of a specific action precisely at that moment when the action occurs? Or, are we disposed to feel a certain way and use that action as an excuse to express said emotion? On the other hand, if we have time to think, would we act in the same way, with the same expression of emotion? In this chapter, I will argue that every human being has an emotional make-up, or what psychologists call 'emotional intelligence,' which is a function of their physiological, linguistic, and cognitive constitution. All of these aspects are found in different degrees and configured in different ways in every human being. There are impulsive types, for instance, who do not think much before they act; there are articulate and inarticulate types who, respectively, express or do not express their emotions linguistically. What I want to propose in this chapter is the necessity of 'emotional maturity' on the part of athletes, a maturity that will be crucial during difficult moments of their sporting activity. This maturity can be developed in training time (see Chapter 5), but its true test will occur during the high stakes game.

Our emotional constitution and its problems stem from ourselves and our interaction with society. Sport is only one arena of human experience, no doubt a unique one, which, depending upon its scope, type, nature, and context, can bring out many intense emotions. Such emotions are not entirely 'made' within the context of sport, but they are 'felt' in sport. Especially in our global age where athletes from different cultures, therefore from different emotional backgrounds and experiences, blend, the total emotional experience becomes hard to understand and disentangle. It becomes even more difficult to do so when emotions are not expressed in any form, which can be due to individual or cultural reasons.

There are many different ways of classifying emotions, but no classification would be definitive, because emotions overlap with one another in many puzzling ways. Spinoza speaks of active vs. passive affects, while Hume divides passions into direct and indirect ones. Psychologists speak of negative and positive emotions as well as low-energy as opposed to high-energy ones. Although Nietzsche and Deleuze do not use these phrases for emotions, we can refer to emotions as being active or reactive. Moreover, we can classify emotions in terms of their objects, whether they are out-side the self or an expression of the self. Finally, we can categorize them according to their level of intensity as in anger vs. rage. These types of classifications, which arise throughout my research, help shed light on the nature of emotions, but cannot categorize them in any strictly definitive manner. Emotions are far more complex and so resist simple classification, not to mention the fact that every human being is a unique configuration of emotions.

In my research, I have benefited from many different schools of philosophy and psychology, even if I do not always agree with their core teachings. I have, for instance, benefited from works that are aligned with cognitive and normative theories, although my main interest for research lies elsewhere. Wherever I found interesting ideas, I explored them. In terms of my inclinations, I have close affinities to existentialism, phenomenology, and psychoanalysis, especially because their approaches to all subjects, including emo-tions, are integral, as they consider all aspects of the human being, do not subscribe to anthropocentric views, do not consider human beings generically as though we are all from the same cut and must fit into the same categories, and, most importantly, place great value on human emotion. I will end my introduction with a list of points that highlight my position on human emotions and which helped me navigate my work on this book:

- Emotion is a state of being that reflects our mental, psychic, and somatic conditions and is connected to such states as feel-ing, sentiment, and affect.
- Emotional conditions reside mostly in our unconscious, which may become conscious depending on one's level of introspection.
- Emotions have different intensities, even if they may be of the same kind.
- Words denoting emotion cannot cover the entire spectrum of emotions; hence, language is not adequate to convey every emotion.
- While the expression of a 'problem emotion' is not the solution of that emotion, a contextualized discharge may help overcome it.
- Every type of emotion needs its own care and cultivation, although every emotion may be said to somehow be related within the character of the same person.
- Ideologies and social bonds may codify specific emotions, the dissolution of which may be more difficult than usual for an

individual to actualize; in other words, emotions have a collective dimension and currency.

Notes

1 I benefitted much from a recent work on Stoicism and emotions, namely, *Die stoische Theorie der Gefühle* by Michael Krewet.
2 In his intro to *Emotions in the Practice of Psychotherapy*, Plutchik lists four theories of emotion – those of Darwin, William James, psychoanalysis, and cognitive theory (2000), but does not mention those developed by philosophers over the centuries. Almost every major school of philosophy has its own theory of emotion.

Bibliography

Darwin, C. (1872/1998). *The Expression of the Emotions in Man and Animals* (ed. by P. Ekman). New York: Oxford University Press.

Descartes, R. (1649/1989). *The Passions of the Soul* (transl. by S. H. Voss). Indianapolis, IN: Hackett.

Goldie, P. (2003). *The Emotions: A Philosophical Exploration*. Oxford: Oxford University Press.

Graver, F. (2007). *Stoicism and Emotion*. Chicago: University of Chicago Press.

Hobbes, T. (1668/1994). *Leviathan* (ed. by E. Curley). Indianapolis, IN: Hackett.

James, W. (1884). 'What is an Emotion?' *Mind* 9:188–205.

Johnston, M. (2001). 'The Authority of Affect'. *Philosophy and Phenomenological Research* 53, 181–214.

Krewet, M. (2013). *Die stoische Theorie der Gefühle*. Heidelberg: Universitätsverlag Winter GmbH Heidelberg.

Plutchik, R. (2000). *Emotions in the Practice of Psychotherapy*. Washington, DC: American Psychological Association.

Spinoza, B. (1989). *Ethics*. (transl. by R. H. M. Elwes). Amherst, NY: Prometheus Books.

Part I

Theoretical framework

In this part, my main task is to establish a framework from which I explore the question of emotion in sport. The topic is vast, studied in both philosophy and psychology, not to mention other fields and is ever-growing for many thinkers and researchers, despite the reflections of many philosophers for more than two millennia. I have chosen four schools of philosophy and ideas related to them from other philosophers: (a) Aristotle's theory of catharsis; within this theory, I examine the need for discharge and externalization for certain emotions; (b) Spinoza's theory of affect in order to understand the rudimentary strata of emotions and their collective aspect; (c) Nietzsche's philosophy of power to examine the place of emotions in power relations, but also understand the feeling of power; (d) Hume's theory of sentiment to investigate the origin and quality of human emotions. While I focus on four fundamental areas (catharsis/discharge, affect/affectivity, power/power relations, and origin/quality) against the theoretical framework I built, there is ample ground in each of these areas where the question of emotion could be posed. In addition to four schools of philosophy, I digress into other philosophers, and psychological and psychoanalytic literature to address/utilize their unique perspectives on the subject.

Chapter 1

Catharsis of emotions

Catharsis in intellectual history

Since Aristotle, catharsis has been part of philosophical debates, but it has also been incorporated into psychological and therapeutic methods. Although the context in which Aristotle presents his theory of catharsis (2002) is drama and the dramatic effect of catharsis on the spectator, which was a counter-response to Plato's ideas on poetry, once its broader meaning is understood, catharsis can be applied to many different fields of human interaction, including sport. Catharsis is often translated as 'purgation,' 'discharge,' or 'purification.' While Aristotle singled out fear and compassion in his theory as primary emotions, every emotion needs to be discharged and, more importantly, its transformation into higher forms. This may be the meaning that lies at the root of 'purification' – for Aristotle, the higher state lies in emotional maturity, which is one of the meanings of *arete* or virtue. This is what broadens his concept of esthetics to the ethical domain. To what end should we purify our emotions? Aristotle's response would be: in order to be the virtuous persons that we can be, to be *megalopyschia*, 'great-souled' individuals.

Plato has less trust than Aristotle in human beings and their random emotional expressions in the public arena; consequently, Plato would rather ban dramatic performances (1992) that had violent scenes in them, suggestive or not, which thereby evoked disturbing emotions in spectators. In addition, he believed such emotions would weaken them and make them poor citizens and soldiers. Plato was more concerned with the order of the state than the emotional well-being of the many. Because his guardians of the state were already, allegedly, emotionally advanced, there was no further need for such emotional therapy at the expense of the state; they were not, for instance, supposed to feel envy (of material goods) or jealousy (of lovers or spouses). In our age, we no longer demarcate the few from the many; therefore, we do not suffer from Plato's anxiety (though we must reflect on it and understand in what ways catharsis can make us weak or strong). The few are blended with the many.

Ultimately catharsis has much to do with healing; this may have been the primary use of the word in religious and medical circles prior to Aristotle. Every emotion, laden with negative energies or potential for negative affects for oneself or others, needs its own care and catharsis. One needs to consider every aspect of a human being to begin the healing process: the mind, the body, the soul, language, etc. More often than not, problems become entangled in the integral human being. Fixing one aspect of the problem is an impartial act of healing.

Nietzsche's response to Aristotle's theory of catharsis is critical; he does not accept catharsis as a fundamental aspect of Greek tragedy because for Nietzsche the Dionysian forms its basis (1967). For Nietzsche the Dionysian is to be connected to all beings, to be able to lose one's self, to recognize one's own mortality, to be nothing, and so on. Although Nietzsche may have a point in distinguishing the Dionysian from catharsis, we cannot reject the latter as a necessary regime of culture. It is one thing to be ecstatic, to lose one's self in the other or in an event, as in a sporting event or a great show, but it is yet another thing to feel emotions, to externalize them, to express them, and to manage or fully live through them. Even though these two, the Dionysian and catharsis, are closely related – aren't we feeling intense emotions when we are ecstatic? – still, they belong to different registers of the human character and culture. Just to illustrate this point, let's keep in mind that one can be emotional but not be Dionysian in the way Nietzsche understood it.

Catharsis played an important role in the early stages of psychoanalysis[1] when Freud and Breuer used hypnotic techniques to release repressed emotions. However, it is important to consider the different versions of catharsis, or what they could mean in specific contexts. I am using the term in a broad way, and always in relation to the care and transformation of emotions into more elevated forms. In the early stages of psychoanalysis, on the other hand, catharsis was a specific method, often used with hypnosis, in order to make patients remember traumatic experiences so that they could revive their repressed memories. For Freud, catharsis connotes experiencing deep emotions, which should be the first step in dealing with any emotional issue. Despite many critics of the cathartic method in psychotherapy, it has many advocates who see value in it, as long as it is properly contextualized (Frank 1971; Janov 1991, 2007; Greenberg 2002).

Contrarily, Bataille focuses on single events in life that can have transformative impact; these are ecstatic moments, and something or someone becomes a trigger, the departure point for such moments. Because, for Bataille, taboos, and transgressions are the undercurrent of human existence, events that transgress taboos are laden with intense emotions. Sport, already of a heterogeneous order belonging to the registers of sacrifice and transgression, is such an ecstatic domain and is rife with emotional experiences. Consider the dismay and grief of defeat, especially in an international game (the Brazilian players and spectators in the 2014 World Cup in Brazil) or joy of victory (when Bolt shows exuberance when winning a race, even though he has won many before) or the anger, disappointment, frustration, or euphoria of thousands of fans screaming in a game. Today, sporting culture, as religious and political ones, contains one of the greatest ecstatic communions of all times.

Sporting context

Sporting events provide outlets to externalize emotions for the entire sporting community. Playing itself, kicking a ball, jumping, and/or punching, can each be a cathartic act. Large games with thousands of spectators and a festival mood can have cathartic effects, too. When the stakes are higher and the collective body larger, as in international games, the emotional barometer also increases to a higher level. These events then become outlets for the emotional expression of all the members of the sporting community. On the one hand, they serve as a discharge for all contained emotions such as anger, frustration, and euphoria. On the other hand, such discharges may become a burden on others. I will discuss the impact of emotional expressions in the chapter on affects, but we cannot forget the context and the limits of our catharsis. One can speak of physical, psychological, mental, and linguistic dimensions of catharsis, all overlapping with each other.

Physical aspect of catharsis

Discharge of emotion can happen physically. Athletes, by virtue of their sporting activity, are constantly discharging their emotions;[2] however, they are bound by the rules of the game they are playing. Therefore, if they have an excess of energies and play too forcefully, they either commit a foul or end up making an action outside the context of their game, which they may find to be cathartic; for instance, Suarez's biting[3] or Zidane's head butt. Even if they are provoked to commit such acts, are they justified in doing so? Their acts are not part of the sporting context and can perpetuate cycles of anger and revenge. However, the excess libido still remains in need of discharging.[4] On the other hand, fans discharge their euphoric emotions of victory or the sadness of defeat as they bond with their team or favorite athlete, although the two primary human emotions Aristotle speaks of in catharsis, compassion and fear (eleos and phobos, often translated as pity and terror), cannot be missing in the economy of the fan's emotions.

There is much discussion in sport literature regarding violence in sport and to what extent it is cathartic and should be acceptable. It is necessary to remember that some sports, such as boxing, martial arts, or American football, are more violent than others, with each sport accepting, or including, certain acceptable forms of aggression or violence. There are different forms of physical contact and violence in different sports. As long as of the rules of each game are obeyed, and athletes are prepared to play against their more or less equals, acts of aggression and violence should be acceptable, which is what some call the social-conventional domain (Bredemeier 1983). Reid and Holowchak disagree with this position: "[T]he data are not unambiguous, current research indicates strongly that exposure to aggression leads not to catharsis, but rather to heightened aggression" (2011: 87). However, we should not forget the *context* of aggression proper to each sport. Clearly, not all aggression should be acceptable, not acts of aggression that are entirely out of context (such as the fights ice hockey players get into, which may be called 'stylized aggression'), not those that are aimed at pleasing an audience hungry for aggression, and not those that are done for commercial reasons. But we cannot dismiss certain appropriate aggressive acts, and their necessity, as in boxing. Do Reid and Holowchak propose to ban boxing, like half of the medical community? Although I agree with their caution on unnecessary or out-of-context aggression in sport, I disagree with the entirety of their position and their conclusion: "[C]ondoning aggression in sport, we contribute to aggression and violence in society" (92). On the contrary, not finding proper means and outlets to express our aggressive instincts, we create more problems for society and we become aggressive toward others in an unjust way. Sport is a place where we can justly externalize our aggression. In short, aggression in sport can be cathartic, both for the athletes and the spectators, as long as aggression remains within the sporting context. I would also go further and maintain that aggression proper to that sport would not invoke negative emotions such as anger and rage, but those that are not proper, out of context, would. What I am suggesting here is this, and there are many studies in this area: (a) every human being needs to discharge his/her emotions; (b) sport is one field where this can happen, wherever we are in the sporting community; (c) there is a discrepancy between players and non-players in their cathartic discharge; (d) this discrepancy needs to be dealt with.

Psychological aspect of catharsis

Athletes, like other human beings, have their own emotional make-up and this can be traced back to their birth, childhood, and developmental process. Athletes bring this psychological strata of their past with them to their sporting practices and culture. Everyone carries psychological strata of this kind, and often, it is inflicted upon those with whom we closely interact. In relationships, our family members often become the recipients of such unworked emotions. Similarly, in sport, the repository of such emotion becomes the sporting community, whether they are our teammates or our opponents. However, it is not wise to treat the sporting community as the targets against whom our 'negative' emotions are discharged, just as it is not fair to discharge such emotions against our friends, lovers, and family members.

Scholars have made many distinctions among the different kinds of aggressions that exist in sports, which members of the sporting community should be alert to. Bredemeier introduces terms such as 'destructive' vs. 'constructive' aggression (in Goldstein 1983: 48). If aggression occurs within the rules of a game and no harm is inflicted upon the opponent, then it is 'constructive aggression.' Parallel to destructive aggression is reactive or angry aggression. One simply acts out of anger and deliberately inflicts harm upon one's opponent *hors de concours*. While physical harm is often inflicted in combat sports, it is not necessarily done out of anger or malice, that is, it is not intentional. On the other hand, athletes may be encouraged to be aggressive so that they can win a game; this type of aggression is called 'instrumental aggression.' One difficulty with these distinctions, if we were to apply them to practice, is not to be able to determine the nature of a particular aggression in the field and its emotional status.

If we are indeed violent and aggressive, for which a discharge is needed, where do such emotions originate? Freud identifies the death drive as the psychic seat of aggression. In the late phase of his works, he calls the death drive an impediment to civilization (1961). Prior to Freud, Adler had come to a similar conclusion and can be considered to be the first, in psychoanalytic theory, to have recognized aggression as an intrinsic aspect of the human psyche.[5] Adler also tries to understand Nietzsche's teachings of power and will to power. What then remained for psychoanalysis to work on were: what lies at the origin of aggression and how it can be dealt with in human life and society? Freud sees frustration and repression at the root of aggression; in his tri-partite topography of the human psyche, all instincts rooted in the id make their demands, but the superego gives permission to some and rejects others. Instincts that are renounced lead to frustration; if a particular instinct/drive is entirely renounced, frustration turns into a chronic form, which can be called 'repression.' The phrase Nietzsche uses for the same phenomenon was the 'internalization' of instincts or 'bad conscience.' (1994). Now, it is not possible to satisfy every single demand of every instinct; however, it is possible to satisfy every type of instinct, if not every single instinct. So, the first question is, and this exceeds the limits of sport, how to deal with repression and the suffering that it can create in the psychic life. The second question concerns how to account for the death drive in such a way that it will not cause more repression and suffering for us and for others. These are both difficult questions, and we are, phylogenetically, far from even getting close to the solution of these two problems. Sport can help alleviate repression and can be an outlet for the externalization of the death drive, as long as the boundaries of aggression are clearly drawn and observed in every type of sport, without leaving much room to the external influences of money and media, both of which concern quantity rather than quality.

Aggression and violence in sport is a major topic today and is something that must be addressed cautiously. I am in firm agreement with Nietzsche's and Freud's conclusions on the necessity for externalizing aggressive instincts, but, of course, *within their appropriate contexts*. However, I will add the following provisos: first, human beings are each different and have different degrees of aggression. The need to externalize such aggression can therefore be more intense with certain individuals. Second, aggression, though understood physically in this context, should not be confined to the physical domain; aggression can be emotional, psychic, linguistic, etc. And aggression and assertion should not be confused with one another. Nonetheless, both assertion and aggression have their place in sport. Third, expressions of aggression in sport need to be promoted and practiced within their own context, which I cannot emphasize sufficiently enough. Fan aggression is entirely out of context and should be prevented at all costs. Finally, and this applies mostly to violent sports, aggression must be contained within the field of sport; for this, athletes need to be specially evaluated and trained. It takes a mature and a cultivated athlete to practice a violent sport but not take such violence outside the sporting context, for instance to his/her household. It is also possible that those who are violently abusive find yet another place in violent sports to vent their aggression.

Finally, I would not disparage athletic aggression in toto. What needs to be done is to prevent physical fan aggression at all costs and to contain athletic aggression to the sporting field itself. On a different note, I disagree with Arendt, who stated that "violence is the expression of impotence" (1969: 32). It depends upon how violence is externalized. Perhaps Arendt had a specific form of aggression in mind when she wrote this. Not all violence is the expression of impotence; what happens when two boxers are violent to each other is part of the nature of the sport they are engaged in. As long as violence occurs between more or less equals and there is a context, it can be 'active' and an expression of active power.

Cognitive aspect of catharsis

One can submit one's raw emotions to one's cognitive process, which entails reflecting, questioning, and thinking so that the problems of raw emotion are exposed and can be transformed into higher emotions. In the spirit of Hume's skepticism, it must be noted that one cannot overcome a problematic emotion solely through cognitive functions. Such a position would neglect the psychosomatic conditions of such emotions. If one has dealt with these deeper conditions, one can also rely on the resources and powers of one's mind and think through difficult emotions. Thinking, arriving at conclusions, or having insights into one's self, can also be cathartic and help us overcome our emotional problems. On the other hand, although I have approached it heuristically here, it is neither easy, nor even desirable, to separate what is cognitive from what is physiological and what is psychical. More often than not, and this should be a running theme all throughout this book, everything that makes us human is integrally enmeshed together and cannot be arbitrarily isolated.

Linguistic aspect of catharsis

Cursing is a common form of discharging contained emotions. It is done in everyday life and in sports, by both athletes and fans alike. Wajnryb highlights three broad contexts for cursing (2005): catharsis, aggression, and social connection. What concerns us here is the first context: we often curse to externalize an emotion. It can be as innocent as saying a curse word to ourselves, or it can be aggressive when used toward someone else. There is no need to exercise politeness about cursing as long as: (a) it is an innocent cursing that involves no one else; (b) it is reciprocal among more or less equals and the cursing will simply remain as cursing, as it does not extend into something else; and (c) it does not stem from lowly character traits or promote such traits. Feezell lists ten different categories of cursing (cathartic, intensifying, expressive, abusive, disparaging, commendatory, lubricating, comedic, subversive, and self-definitional) and agrees with Wajnryb "when she claims that this [cathartic] kind of cussing is the most straightforward" (2008: 22). I agree with Feezell's argument (2008) against O'Connor (2006) that cursing can be cathartic and therefore positive.

Further on Aristotle on emotion

I would like to add two more themes here as they could help us better understand Aristotle's ideas on emotion. First, his discussion of emotion in relation to the ideal of excellence; and second, the collective dimension of emotion. Aristotle presents his theory of *arete* (translated as virtue or excellence) in relation to feeling and one's/

the capacity to feel. An excellent person, in his account, knows how to turn negative emotions into positive ones (*Nicomachean Ethics*, Book I); therefore, for Aristotle, being virtuous is immediately connected with what he calls right emotions and the right emotional state of being: "[V]irtues are concerned with actions and feelings, and every feeling and every action entails pleasure and pain. That is also why virtue is concerned with pleasures and pains" (2014: 24). Although Aristotle's emphasis on the primacy of pleasure and pain cannot be taken for granted, his general point that excellence demands a specific emotional make-up and a specific emotional response to action cannot be dismissed. Feeling, capacity, and state (or disposition) are all related by way of virtue. Pain and pleasure are primordial in the sense that all emotions can be traced back to them: "By feelings," Aristotle says, "I mean appetite, anger, fear, confidence, envy, enjoyment, love, hatred, longing, jealousy, pity, and generally whatever entails pleasure and pain" (2014: 26). Do all feelings entail pleasure and pain? Does our emotional make-up start and end with pleasure and pain? I will return to these questions when I explore Nietzsche's ideas on this topic, for he brings an alternative perspective to it.

On the other hand, emotions live in their own domain and they resonate with its elements. Like in familial relations, people in proximity know what would arouse their emotions in what direction. For instance, we can disturb the emotions of a just judge in such a way that he or she can no longer exact justice, as Aristotle illustrates: "It is not right to pervert the judge by moving him to anger or envy or pity – one might as well warp a carpenter's rule before using it" (1994: Book I, section 1). Even someone who is well meaning can be emotionally agitated by others and act in a disturbed way. In sport, players and umpires can be provoked in many different ways. This again shows the necessity of caring for our emotions in some way, which the theory of catharsis suggests. If we discharge our emotions properly/rightly, we will not be so easily agitated and therefore be less prone to negatively violent outbursts. Alternatively, we may also question the agitator and his/her motives.

Chapter conclusion

At the core of the cathartic regimen lies the need to *transfigure* our destructive instincts and urges into positive, uplifting experiences, and not simply to vent our emotions without context; in other words, to turn 'bad Eris' into 'good Eris,' to use Nietzsche's phrase by way of his reading of Hesiod (1976: 35), to transform lower emotions into higher ones.[6] Although this may be a Herculean task, the vision of such transfiguration must be kept alive so that the sporting culture thrives in uplifting emotions, which many athletes still seek to achieve. Every member of the sporting community must channel his/her raw emotions into those that are sublime for a higher quality of emotional expressions, as they must be cognizant of the affects they create in specific power relations. Even though they are not exactly the same, Freud's idea of sublimation overlaps with Nietzsche's notion of transfiguration (the term "sublimation" is also used by Nietzsche). For Freud (1961), sublimation is the process of transforming libido into cultural activities and achievements such as arts and sciences, but we can add sports here as well (though discussion of sport is hardly present in Freud).

In my discussion in this chapter, I did not make clear distinctions among different members of the sporting community in relation to catharsis. Clearly, they each follow a different pathway in terms of their catharsis. While Aristotle focuses on the spectator in his catharsis theory, I have put the emphasis on the players. They are the primary beneficiaries of psychosomatic catharsis, while the spectators are bereft of the physical actions of the sporting field. Much analysis of catharsis has, however, revolved around spectators, with many studies concluding that sport spectators like to see aggression in sport and that it is presumably cathartic for them. The media simply caters to such demands while owners and managers are interested in numbers (higher number of viewers, spectators in the stadium, etc.) because they bring in more revenue. These factors, whether financial or 'spectacular,' I find to be extrinsic and destructive to the spirit of sport.

Notes

1 For an overview of ideas on catharsis from Aristotle until recent times, see Gordon W. Russell's 'Psychological Issues in Sport Aggression,' *Violence in Sport* (Goldstein 1983).
2 One can ask if sport is physically cathartic for professional players because they play all the time and playing has become their primary nature. Do they still feel the discharge if they play almost habitually?
3 See Martinková and Parry's essay, 'On Biting in Sport – The Case of Luis Suárez,' for an extensive analysis of this incident and for their argument as to why such out-of-context acts are not acceptable in sport, or in soccer in this case.

4 Different types of sport can induce different levels of physical catharsis.
   We should also not forget individual differences and the varying needs
   for physical catharsis. Some may need catharsis more than others. For
   athletes who have excess libido and cannot discharge it in their type of
   sport, they will have to find other ways to do so, rather than burden their
   field with their excess libidinal energies.
5 In this context, we must also add Melanie Klein and her followers,
   who view aggression as more fundamental than any other psychical
   phenomena.
6 By supporting the need for catharsis or the transfiguration of emotions in
   sport, I do not, in any way, subscribe to the functionalist theory of sport,
   let alone reduce sport to this function. Sport could then just become
   a medium for such transfiguration for some members of the sporting
   community, but this is not its primary function or nature. For different
   theories of sport, see Robert L. Simon's 'Theories of Sport' (Torres 2014).

Bibliography

Arendt, H. (1969). *On Violence*. New York: Harcourt Brace Jovanovich.

Aristotle (1994). *On Rhetoric: A Theory of Civic Discourse* (transl. by G.
Kennedy). New York: Oxford University Press.

———. (2002). *Poetics*. (transl. by S. Benardete and M. Davis). South Bend,
IN: St. Augustine Press.

———. (2014). *Nicomachean Ethics*. (transl. by C. D. C. Reeve). Indianapolis, IN: Hackett Publishing Co.

Bataille, G. (1985). *Visions of Excess*. (transl. by Allan Stoekl). Minneapolis, MN: University of Minnesota Press.

Bredemeier, B. J. (1983). 'Athletic Aggression: A Moral Concern'. In J. H.
Goldstein (ed.), *Sports Violence* (pp. 47–82). New York: Springer-Verlag.

Feezell, R. (2008). 'Vulgarians of the World Unite: Sport, Dirty Language,
and Ethics'. *Journal of the Philosophy of Sport* 35:1, 17–42.

Frank, J. D. (1971). 'Therapeutic Factors in Psychotherapy'. *Journal of Psychotherapy* 25, 350–361.

Freud, S. (1961). *Civilization and Its Discontents*. (ed. by J. Strachey). New
York: W. W. Norton.

Goldstein, J. H. (ed.). (1983). *Sports Violence*. New York: Springer-Verlag.

Greenberg, L. S. (2002). *Emotion-Focused Therapy*. Washington, DC:
American Psychological Association.

Holowchak, M. A. (2011). 'Freud on Play, Games, and Sports Fanaticism'.
*Journal of the American Academy of Psychoanalysis and Dynamic Psy-
chiatry* 39:4, 695–716.

Janov, A. (1991). *The New Primal Scream: Primal Therapy 20 Years On*.
Blair, NE: Enterprise Publishing.

———. (2007). *Primal Healing*. Franklin Lakes, NJ: Career Press.

Martinková, I. and Parry, J. (2015). 'On Biting in Sport: The Case of Luis
Suárez'. *Sport, Ethics, and Philosophy* 9:2, 214–232.

Nietzsche, F. (1967). *The Birth of Tragedy*. (transl. by W. Kaufmann). New York: Vintage Press.

———. (1976). *The Portable Nietzsche*. (transl. by W. Kaufmann). New York: Penguin Books.

———. (1994). *On the Genealogy of Morals*. (transl. by W. Kaufmann). New York: Vintage Press in Basic Writings of Nietzsche edited by W. Kaufmann.

O'Connor, J. V. (2006). *Cuss Control: The Complete Book on How to Curb Your Cussing*. New York: iUniverse.

Plato. (1992). *The Republic*. (ed. by C. D. C. Reeve and transl. by G. M. A. Grube). Indianapolis, IN: Hackett Publishing Co.

Reid, H. and Holowchak, M. (2011). *Aretism: An Ancient Sports Philosophy for the Modern Sports World*. Lanham, MD: Lexington Books.

Torres, C. (2014). *The Bloomsbury Companion to the Philosophy of Sport*. London: Bloomsbury.

Wajnryb, R. (2005). *Expletive Deleted: A Good Look at Bad Language*. New York: Free Press.

Chapter 2

The question of affect-impact and collective dimension of emotions

Spinoza may be considered to be the first philosopher to take human emotions seriously who rightly observed that "no one . . . has defined the nature and strength of the emotions" (1989: 127). The term Spinoza uses for 'emotion' is *affekt*, often translated as 'affect' in English; however, these two terms, though related, cover different fields. The emphasis in Spinoza's version of emotion theory is the ability to make changes or to influence, especially because emotion is indicative of change in one's disposition. 'Affect' and 'effect' are somewhat related; effects are those aspects of events that can be more known than affects. This makes the former the subject matter of metaphysics and the latter that of psychology. Affects, understood as emotions, remain unknown to a large extent, and this remains to be a human mystery. Even the most introspective persons are not fully cognizant of the affects they create. What follows below is an exploration of Spinoza's teachings, how they were later adapted into philosophy, and what they could mean in the sport context.

Emotion is modification of the body. When an emotion is felt, the active power of the said body is increased or diminished (1989: 129). If I feel anger, something changes in my bodily disposition (in organ functions, respiration, heartbeat, facial expression, body posture, hand gestures, etc.). Darwin's work (1872/1998) on facial expressions and other studies in this area can shed much light on the visible and invisible physiological changes that occur when we experience an emotion.

It is hard to control strong emotions (1989: 133). Control of emotions has been a hotly contested topic among philosophers. As mentioned before, the Stoics believed that a good Stoic can and should control his emotions. This is easier said than done. First, the Stoics did not make a distinction among the multitude of emotions (they included only a few); second, how desirable is it to be controlling emotions at all times and in every context? And what does control mean? In psychoanalysis, control could be indicative of repression or a strong defense mechanism, which keeps the emotions hidden and repressed. There are times when we need to be fearful so that we can survive; there are other times when we have to feel the force of ambition so that we can strive for higher goals. Spinoza's point and his acceptance of mind/body integration are far more insightful than the Stoic position.

Emotion vs. action. "Every one shapes his actions according to his emotion. . . . All these considerations clearly show that a mental decision and a bodily appetite, or determined state, are simultaneous, or rather one and the same thing . . ." (1989: 133). There is an interesting dynamic between action and emotion; actions often provoke emotional responses and intense emotions such as anger, jealousy, and revenge, which can incite people to action. An extensive discussion of this topic is to be found in the last chapter of this book.

Furthermore, there are three primary emotions in Spinoza (1989: 138): desire, pleasure, and pain. All other emotions arise from these three.[1] Desire is appetite with consciousness thereof. Pleasure takes one toward perfection, higher states, and leads to an increase in vitality, whereas pain is the opposite, leading to a decrease in vitality. I do not see how desire can be a specific emotion and Spinoza seems to be grappling with this issue, as he sometimes identifies desire with pleasure. Desire can be the seat of all emotions, similar to the libido for Freud.

Several emotions may come together, forming a compound (1989: 174). Spinoza does not indicate the limitations of linguistic expression, but this may be in the background of his thought (1989: 135). There are many mixed emotional states for which language does not have any words, which can even reflect opposing emotions. I may have love and hate for the same person at the same time, and these emotions may pull me in opposite directions. Such mixed or confused emotional states can be described as 'undecidable' or 'chiasmatic' or 'uncanny.'[2]

What we find in Spinoza's theory of affect is not so much the control of emotions as their introspective understanding. As Totaro notes: "Spinoza's theory of affects thus marks the abandonment of an interpretive model that identifies passion with vice or a weakness to fight or overcome, and considers the affects instead as building blocks at the foundation of the essence of the individual" (2017: 225). Affects, which stand for a variety of related physical and mental phenomena, can manifest themselves inwardly or outwardly. Lastly, there is no causal link between a concealed interior and a visible exterior.

Much of Spinoza's theory of affect can be read as a response to Descartes' theory of passions. Descartes treats passions as willful activities of the mind. In his *Passions of the Soul*, Descartes considers the body to be passive (the receptor of emotion, nonetheless) and the mind to be the active and main source of all emotions. Therefore, his remedy to the problems of emotional disturbance is the mental control of emotions, similar to what the Stoics propose: "This remedy calls for a proper use of memory and a constant exercise of emotional detachment" (Totaro 2017: 236) and Descartes finds fault with the senses and imagination (Descaretes 1989: Part III). Descartes assumes, disregarding the psychosomatic roots of human emotions, that one can somehow choose the right emotion. At the end of his *Passions*, he confirms that we can dominate our emotional lives. Spinoza does not agree with this willful solution of Descartes, but rather proposes an affective remedy, which "consists in a cognitive acquisition" (Totaro 2017: 241), relying on the internal goodness of the human being and the different levels of knowledge that reside in reason, one of which constitutes the true knowledge of affects themselves. Much of Spinoza's reflection revolves around deciphering the nature of affects and emotions, rather than their control or cure.

Shared emotions in sport

Feelings are not *spontaneous* as is often claimed; we *feel* in relation to our own being and what we are experiencing. Here we must keep in mind the collective aspect of the sporting culture; most fans act out of the herd instinct. The masses that they belong to exert a weight upon them. Perhaps left alone they would not act in this way, but now there is a show, there is a chain reaction among the members of their fandom. This, of course, opens up the question of collective emotions, or 'shared emotions' as Mikko Salmela calls them. "When individuals identify with a group or think of themselves in terms of a particular social identity, they can experience 'group-based emotions' when something relevant happens to their in group or salient social identity" (e.g. Kessler and Hollbach 2005;

Smith, Seger, and Mackie 2007; Salmela 2012). In most human interactions, including sports, we do not *feel* and express our *own* emotions, but rather those of others or other groups. No doubt, these emotions can be traced back to some human origin, but they get lost in the communal forms of being. The act of catharsis can then become convoluted to say the least, or misguided. It is no longer my discharge but rather a collective discharge; and in this sense, one can question to what extent such catharsis can contribute to the well-being of the individual, although 'authentic' catharsis could. This takes us to the question of affect and power: what are the kinds of affects we create in ourselves and on others and what forms of power do we exercise?

The idea of collective emotion can be explained by way of 'affectivity' in Spinoza. "The recognition of an emotional response similar to that of another man is, however, a prerequisite for the establishment of an affective activity that characterizes us as human beings" (Totaro 2017: 239). Although the context in which this is presented is *pietas* and suffering, the idea of affectivity applies to every emotion. Affectivity works within the resonance of the same or similar types and situations; it is based on the imagination of the similarity between our situation and that of our fellow human beings. A similar fate is binding for each community; in sport, all the fans feel united with themselves and with their team. If their team wins, they all win. Similar emotions then resonate in that community, as they do among members of close relations.

Affect and power

Spinoza is the first major thinker to develop a theory of affect and includes in this theory an extensive discussion of emotions. An affect, within the human realm, is the impact of an action or sensation on someone with the potentiality of engendering a response. We produce affects all the time through different media, sometimes consciously but, more often than not, unconsciously. We are often unaware of the affects our actions create on others. What we say may hurt others, although we had no intention for any harm. In the public arena, respected figures have more impact on their followers because of their position. This leads us to the question of power, and this is one aspect of Nietzsche's philosophy of power that was inspired by Spinoza's theory of affect.

For Nietzsche "the will to power is the primitive form of affect, that all other affects are only developments of it" (*The Will to Power*, section 688). Life is power, whatever has life has affect, the will to power even in its most rudimentary form has affect; therefore, we can say that organs, drives, instincts, and psychic functions also have affects; all other affects develop out of these rudimentary affects. Now, we have a theory of affect and philosophy of power built from fundamental physiological functions. The desire to bite someone may be a basic animal instinct, but has no place in soccer; its affect on other players and the soccer community can be detrimental. Therefore, such a basic instinct needs to be channeled into another arena. Such actions may provoke a chain of negative reactions, which will ruin the spirit of sport. In a similar vein, game-fixing, racial and ethnic prejudices, misjudgment on the part of coaches and umpires, and one-sided use of performance enhancement drugs can and often do have negative affects and produce negative feelings in the players and the spectatorship. Affects are produced in a community, which is similar to what Salmela calls 'shared emotions.'

Furthermore, we can consider affects as active or reactive, following Nietzsche's use of these terms, as I have done within the context of soccer (2017):

Problem 3: *Affects: Active vs. Reactive.* In every spectacular event, affects are re-produced at small or great scales. The question to examine here is what those affects are and how, in what context, are they produced? For the sake of simplicity, I would like to split affects into two: internal affects and external affects. By internal affects, I mean those affects that are produced according to the rules of the game. A beautiful shot into the goalie or the way a goal-keeper jumps and kicks the ball away, which could easily have been a goal. Those sport actions that are unique, unusual, spontaneous, and over-humanly invoke awe and inspiration on the part of the spectators. By external affects, I mean those affects that are produced at a game but are not according to the rules of the game. For instance, the incident at the 2014 World Cup when Uruguay's Luiz Suarez bit into the shoulder of Italy's defender Giorgio Chiellini. Or, the head butt of France's Zidane against Italy's Marco Materazzi at 2006 World Cup. They clearly belong to the event[3] of the game, but they produce different kinds of affects. I would argue that these types of external affects often produce reactive affects. It opens up more divisiveness among players and among opposing fans of the teams and do not cultivate feelings that are appropriate to the spirit of sport.

(Tuncel 2017: 182)

The examples I gave are for affects that were produced among players in the sporting field. There are also affects produced between spectators and players. In Europe many soccer players of African origin have become subject to racist insults and invectives; clearly such racist acts do not stem from soccer itself and produce negative affects. Let's remember that affects, whether positive or negative, are contagious, because they work at the most primordial level of psychosomatic registers. This is why it is hard to eliminate socio-cultural malaises. Unless they are worked out at the level of their 'affectivity,' it is unlikely that they will be entirely eliminated. Political correctness or the censoring words are facile solutions and will not help to eradicate deep-seated prejudices.

Psychoanalytic theory of affects

What stands out in the psychoanalytic theory of affect is its holistic approach: "Affects are complex phenomena that include (a) sensations of pleasure and unpleasure, or a mixture of the two and (b) thoughts, memories, and wishes – in a word, ideas. Ideas and sensation together constitute an affect" (Brenner 1980: 343). What is also significant is the emphasis this theory places on the unconscious processes[4]; namely that both sensations and ideas remain wholly or partly unconscious. This is why subjective data are not always reliable – Brenner splits data into three types: subjective (common to human beings), behavioral (voluntary control and physiological functions), and ethological (related to animals); in other words, human beings are not introspective about their emotions, or more significantly, about their repressed emotions (emotions that are determined, to a large extent, through repression).

Furthermore, Brenner examines two assumptions in Freud regarding affects (Freud 1915, 1919): first, each affect can be clearly differentiated from every other as observed in each individual. Second, affects that correspond to processes of instinctual discharge or gratification are to be understood in quantitative terms (Brenner 1980: 342–343) – it must be noted at the outset that for Freud affects are not repressed, but rather ideas are, and the affects attached to them are displaced (this will be further discussed in Chapter 9). Brenner disagrees with the first; according to him it is not possible to distinguish affects as clearly as it has been assumed so far and affects cannot be uniform from one individual to the next. As for the second assumption, Brenner accepts it but adds the importance of psychic development in the development of affects. Regarding the ontogeny of affect, Brenner follows the main teachings of psychoanalysis: "[E]ach affect has its beginning early in life when ideas first become associated with sensations of pleasure and unpleasure" (343). Such sensations are associated with instinctual drives, their tension, and discharge, that is, whether they are satisfied or not. It follows from all of this that the psychic development, the formation of ego/id/superego constellation, corresponds to the 'affective' and emotional development of a person.

Some of the lessons that can be derived from psychoanalytic teachings are as follows: affects are partly or wholly unconscious – Deleuze (1983) considers affects to be entirely pre-conscious – ; they are the unconscious conditions of possibility of emotions and feelings; they are associated with sensations, their intensity, and ideas; they vary from individual to individual and culture to culture. Each affect is unique for each individual. These differences can be attributed to the different physiological, psychic, and mental constitution and their different developmental processes. Finally, there are mixed affects as well, with each mixture also being unique to each individual and culture.

I will extend the psychoanalytic theory of emotion by making two distinctions: (a) between emotion and feeling (as they relate to the unconscious); and (b) between what is episodic and what is dispositional. At the end, I hope to tie all of these terms together and link them to the theory of affect. Feelings are the windows of more unconscious emotions; however, it would not be inconsistent to say that they can be both conscious and unconscious. Feelings extend downwards from consciousness to unconsciousness while emotions shoot upwards. For instance, when I feel angry at someone, I am aware of my feeling. But the psychosomatic conditions for my anger rest in the deeper strata of my unconscious, which we can call the 'emotion of anger,' a more permanent state than the feeling itself, which is momentary. This emotion is rooted in the topographic components of my psyche, a great part of which is the id (the seat of drives, which is wholly unconscious). We can understand this emotion, and any other emotion, as it emerges from the dynamics of our unique id/ego/superego constitution and their internal relationship. Every drive manifests itself differently, depending upon its nature and pace, and the id can find itself mostly if not entirely unsatisfied, which often leads to frustration. This can happen where the superego reigns supreme and does not give in to the demands of the id, even if they are 'legitimate.' What I am getting into here is the chronically angry person; however, anyone can become angry depending upon the context. This brings us to the second distinction I made previously between the episodic and the dispositional.

Following the aforementioned example, one can be chronically angry, which is dispositional, or one can become in the proper context, that is, from one episode to another. In both cases, the emotion of anger is seated primarily in the unconscious. What then is the difference between the two? In the latter case, one's emotional response is based on context; one does not get angry at anything or most things, or arbitrarily, but rather in a fitting context. But, to play the devil's advocate, one could say that there are things that would make any human being angry, things that are specific to them and their personality type. How different is this episodic anger from dispositional anger? The difference, in my view, lies in 'what' one gets angry at and 'how' that anger manifests itself, that is, in the 'affectivity' of the emotion. I would also add, perhaps with caution, that the chronically angry person is less conscious of the true source of his or her anger than the one who is episodically angry; the former has more to deal with in her unconscious than the latter.

Some have argued against the idea of unconscious emotion in psychoanalysis. One such argument runs as follows:

> Psychoanalysis conceives of mental states in terms of thought contents, or affects, or, as in the case of emotions, of combinations of mental content and affect. The process of repression effects a dissociation of the thought from the affective energy originally attached to its content. Hence, the thought is kept in the unconscious and the affect either dissipates or acquires a different form. . . . Consequently we can no longer speak of an emotion being (in the) unconscious.
>
> (Hatzimoysis 2007: 293)

What this argument keeps out of the picture is all the psychosomatic processes that are formed at pre- or non-linguistic levels and that the unconscious origin of human emotions are rooted in those processes. Associations may dissolve between affects and thoughts, but image-symbol relations, which are primordial, often remain knotted in the registers of the human soul. The phrase 'unconscious emotion' may be confusing, because when we feel an emotion, we are conscious of that emotion; however, the main psychoanalytic position would be that our emotions are grounded in unconscious forces and processes, most of which remain unknown to us most of the time. Even if some of them become conscious, more remains unconscious. This is the crux of the issue. Even the most introspective person has not dealt with the unconscious origin of all of his/ her emotions. That would be a Herculean task indeed. We can hope that human beings are on the path of such introspection; on the other hand, if leaders, parents, teachers, etc. are emotionally immature, such introspective moves will not only happen but will be retarded further, and our unique emotional configuration will remain tangled to us.

To return to the previous argument, if affective energies are all diffused, not everything is diffused; primordial image-symbol relations reappear in different forms while carrying on the same initial emotion. One meaning of repetition is this: that the initial emotion repeats itself in different moments, contexts, and episodes. This knotted emotion will not change unless the person undergoes some deep transformation in and through therapy or self-therapy. That is when that knot can dissolve; a cathartic or an affective event can trigger the change. We cannot look at the subject of 'unconscious emotion' only at the level of thought and affect, especially if the latter excludes images and symbols and includes only physiological forces. We are often conscious of the emotions we feel with the exception of certain cases such as alexithymia, but are often unconscious of their origin, that is, the psychosomatic conditions that made these emotions possible. I will also add that not every emotion needs to be subject to psychoanalytic intervention or therapy.

To conclude: Affect is the non-conscious experience of intensity; affect is hard to grasp because it is pre-linguistic or extra-linguistic. It is the body's predisposition or 'grammar' so to speak. The infant has no prior experience to feel or language to express that feeling; for the infant, affect is emotion. However, for the adult, affect is what makes feelings feel. Affect is what determines both the quantity and the quality of a feeling. Affect always precedes and can be said to be the a priori condition for emotions and feelings. But how are affects transmitted? This is what Spinoza called 'affection.' Because affects are unformed, they can be transmitted from one body to another even unbeknownst to the person. This is not to say that emotions and feelings are transmitted in the same way, but rather, their conditions are transmitted. This is why what is of utmost importance are the kinds of affects that are produced and how they are transmitted in the domain of the collective unconscious, as, for instance, in media and in all types of spectacles (Deleuze, *Thousand Plateaus* by way of Brian Massumi).

Conclusion

There are deeper conditions that lie at the root of many of our feelings and emotions. Just to revisit the issue of semantics, it is not wrong, in my view, to say, for instance, that anger is an affect, an emotion, and a feeling. All these words reveal the different levels or depths of the emotion itself. The theory of affect, instigated by Spinoza and later taken on by Nietzsche, Freud, psychoanalysis, and Deleuze (each in his own manner), goes to this root. Why we feel this way or that way, why we burst out in anger at a teammate or why we always look for a guilty party when the problem in question may be collective, that we ourselves may be implicated in the problem; all of these emotional problems, the root of which often remains unknown to the person and which can adversely affect the spirit of playing must be sought in the psychosomatic development of individuals, in the unconscious layers of the economy of their drives and instincts, the social acceptance of these problematic emotions and the psychic developments associated with them. Affect almost always connotes this depth in the human soul and the rise and fall of its undercurrents, as they guide one's disposition and let it burst open in different episodes.

Notes

1 In addition to pleasure and pain, Spinoza uses love and hate when he defines emotions; love and hate are derived, respectively, from pleasure and pain (1989: 140).
2 There are many possible combinations of emotions, but the ones that pull the psyche apart can have a tremendous emotional toll from which the person who feels it may not pull through.
3 For a discussion of the concept of event, see Grant Farred's book *In Motion, At Rest: The Event of the Athletic Body.* (Minneapolis: University of Minnesota Press, 2014).

4 I must include here another approach to 'affect,' that is common in cognitive psychology. Here is a sample: "Affect, also referred to as *core affect*, is the basic subtrata of consciousness, its most elementary constituent" (Eklund and Tenenbaum 2014: 16). I would have said it is the basic substrata of unconsciousness. The description, however, continues with what we may attribute to unconscious processes: "Affect has a distinctive experiential quality that does not consist of nor require cognition or reflection. It is an inherent and necessary ingredient of emotions and moods . . ." The author suggests that affects are farther removed from the rational, and are connected to emotions and moods. So far, I find this accurate. Then he writes: "Rather, it is always accessible to conscious awareness . . ." I would rather suggest that affects are rarely and hardly or with difficulty accessible to conscious awareness. They are deeply rooted in our physiological functions and psychic registers, or even better in our psychosomatic constitution, because we are neither solely physical nor solely psychical beings. I write this last part in response to a possible question such as this one: "Aren't you conscious of a physiological state like exhaustion or hunger?" Well, our psychosomatic constitution is way more complex than such states. And affects cannot be understood in strictly physiological terms.

Bibliography

Brenner, C. (1980). 'Psychoanalytic Theory of Affect'. In R. Plutchik and H. Kellerman (eds.), *Emotion: Theory, Research and Experience* (pp. 341–348). New York: Academic Press.

Darwin, C. (1872/1998). *The Expression of the Emotions in Man and Animals.* (ed. by P. Ekman). New York: Oxford University Press.

Deleuze, G. (1983). *Nietzsche & Philosophy.* (transl. by H. Tomlinson). New York: Columbia University Press.

Descartes, R. (1649/1989). *The Passions of the Soul.* (transl. by S. H. Voss). Indianapolis, IN: Hackett Publishing Co.

Eklund, R. C. and Tenenbaum, G. (2014). *Encyclopedia of Sport and Exercise Psychology.* London: SAGE Publications.

Farred, G. (2014). *In Motion, At Rest: The Event of the Athletic Body.* Minneapolis, MN: University of Minnesota Press.

Freud, S. (1915). *Standard Edition of the Complete Psychological Works of Sigmund Freud* (Vol. 14). (ed. by J. Strachey). London: Hogarth Press.

———. (1919). *Standard Edition of the Complete Psychological Works of Sigmund Freud* (Vol. 17). (ed. by J. Strachey). London: Hogarth Press.

Hatzimoysis, A. (2007). 'The Case against Unconscious Emotions'. *Analysis* 67:4, 292–299.

Kessler, T., and Hollbach, S. (2005). 'Group-based Emotions as Determinants of Ingroup Identification'. *Journal of Experimental Social Psychology* 41:6, 677–685.

Nietzsche. F. (1967). *The Will to Power.* (transl. by W. Kaufmann). New York: Vintage Press.

Salmela, M. (2012). 'Shared Emotions'. *Philosophical Explorations: An International Journal for the Philosophy of Mind and Action* 15:1, 33–46.

Smith, E. R., Seger, C. R., and Mackie, D. M. (2007). 'Can Emotions Be Truly Group Level? Evidence Regarding Four Conceptual Criteria.' *Journal of Personality and Social Psychology* 93:3, 431–446.

Spinoza, B. (1989). *Ethics*. (transl. by R. H. M. Elwes). Amherst, NY: Prometheus Books.

Totaro, P. (2017). 'The Terminology of the Affects in Ethics Parts III through V'. In Y. Y. Melamed (ed.), *Spinoza's Ethics*. Cambridge: Cambridge University Press.

Tuncel, Y. (2017). 'The Aesthetic and Ecstatic Dimensions of Soccer: Towards a Philosophy of Soccer'. *Soccer & Society* 18:2–3, 181–187.

Chapter 3

The feeling of power and power relations

It is often argued that power is not a feeling or an emotion. If it is an emotion, of all the emotions that we typically have, which would it be? Well, it may not be an emotion, but it is a feeling insofar as we *do feel* in relation to our place in power relations. We feel powerful or not and such feelings do bear on our emotional composition. The feeling of power works from the ground up, from affects toward emotions, and every emotion that is felt and expressed has a relationship to the feeling of power. Furthermore, power relations, one's place in those relations, and the forms of power that are operative in these relations, often remain unspoken or cloaked in social positions. This chapter will address the question of power, the feeling of power, and both the feeling of power and forms of power can contribute to our understanding of emotion in general and emotion in sport.

The feeling of power (*Machtsgefühl*)

I will first highlight the basic aspects of Nietzsche's philosophy of power, then move on to his later teachings on the will to power and finally on active vs. reactive forms of power. In his early and mid-period writings, prior to *Thus Spoke Zarathustra*, Nietzsche reflects on *Machtsgefühl*, the 'feeling of power,' a primordial state of being that is connected to the deeper registers of the human soul and body such as pain and pleasure, the rudimentary instincts and drives. That power is pervasive and we are all in power relations is a point that is present implicitly or explicitly in Nietzsche's writings. I cite *Daybreak* Aphorism 189 to support this thesis. Many of these early reflections on power have to do with joy and suffering and how these feelings are expressed in and through power relations.

"for to practice cruelty is to enjoy the highest gratification of the feeling of power" (1982: 18). That human beings are cruel and that cruelty is a part of our psyche is a point Nietzsche often brings up; however, here the emphasis is on power and how expressions of cruelty, more open in archaic societies and more subtly with us, are ways of feeling and exercising power – that we have become subtle with power is mentioned in *Daybreak* 23: "But because the feeling of impotence and fear was in a state of almost continuous stimulation so strongly and for so long, the *feeling of power* has evolved to such a degree of subtlety. [. . .]" Clearly, in sports many cruel acts are accepted – the degree of cruelty depends upon the type of sport, or what may be constituted as cruel ordinarily – and many of these acts are in conformity with the spirit of sport. Many basic human emotions are connected with this feeling of power; some of the most oft-discussed feelings in Nietzsche include pity, compassion, empathy, punishment, guilt, no-guilt (in relation to blaming and its opposite, praising) and the like. For instance, Nietzsche sees blaming and praising as outlets for the feeling of power to discharge itself. "Guilt is always sought wherever there is failure; for failure brings with it a depression of spirits against which the sole remedy is instinctively applied: a new excitation of the *feeling of power*. . . . Whether we are *praised* or *blamed* what we usually constitute are opportunities . . ." (1982: 88). Attributing guilt is a common trend in sports, especially in cases of defeat, which Nietzsche diagnoses as an expression of power. Clearly, whoever attributes guilt attempts to establish power over the so-called 'guilty.' In many cases, such things happen so subtly that a power relation seems to be absent; this, however, is far from being the case. On a final note from Nietzsche's early reflections, he speaks of the Golden Mean and how important it is to recognize one's place in power relations although it is dynamic and ever-changing. Nietzsche warns his readers against powerlessness and power lust because they are equally problematic. What is necessary is to recognize that we are in power relations. Because that is the case, we must *know* how to handle power in its multiple, matrix-like structures, and in its shifting dynamics and, as I shall discuss later, to exercise *active* forms of power. One has to *know* not only how to seek and attain power but also how to rescind it; those who suffer from fear of power cannot do the former and those who have power lust cannot achieve the latter. Human life is strung across these two problematic existential states of power relations.

Nietzsche's doctrine of the will to power as presented in *Zara-thustra* and its aftermath (including his *Nachlass*) is a conglomeration of many of his ideas on power, most of which are agonistic in spirit. Now I will discuss the agonistic aspects of the will to power. First of all, what Zarathustra learns from life on power (*Zarathustra* II, 'Self-Overcoming') is that power is about 'obeying and commanding'; that is, it is about a hierarchy whether it is within the individual himself or herself or within a community. As for the latter, the sporting hierarchy consists of trainers, coaches, teachers, umpires, referees, and organizers. It is important to remember here that competition takes place in a highly hierarchical world although the contest itself occurs among more or less equals. Even if there is less of a hierarchy among athletes, one can still talk about a relation of obeying and commanding among them as one athlete or team is ahead of the other in the game and commands in this way. The second agonistic teaching of life has to do with the desire to be master; in contest this is the desire to be the victor. In winning the contest, the victor has gained mastery over his or her weaknesses and also over the weaker contestants. Third, the weak have to serve the strong; the losing contestants must accept their defeat and look up to the strong. Here the mythic hierarchy facilitates the acceptance of defeat, as I argued in my essay, 'Defeat, Loss, Death, and Sacrifice in Sport' (2013), because all contestants, the strong and the weak, look up to their gods and heroes as exemplary models of strength. The fourth teaching has to do with self-overcoming: "I am that which must always overcome itself." Life is overcoming, human is that which has to be overcome toward the Overhuman. In contest one is always striving to be higher than what one already is, at least, until the end of the actual contest. The idea of transforming oneself as one strives higher, which is one of the meanings of the *Übermensch*, is already an agonistic idea. The fifth teaching of life is that it is oppositional: 'Whatever I create and however much I love it – soon I must oppose it and my love; thus my will wills it' (*Zarathustra* II, 'Self-Overcoming'). Opposition is the fuel for self-overcoming; the contestant opposes not only his enemies in strife but also the prize itself if he becomes the victor, as was the case with the ancient Greek athlete. He rescinds the prize for his city-state and her gods. He cannot remain as the permanent victor. On the one hand, the victor can always be displaced in the next round; on the other hand, because of this possibility of loss, the victor is compelled to continue with his discipline and training. In this way contest renews itself along with the contestants. Here lies the importance of competition as a process of renewal, a process in which power flows and power dynamics are constantly shifting.

Finally, Nietzsche's conception of active power (in general, the concepts of 'active' and 'reactive') can shed light on the form of power and the kinds of affects we reproduce in the way we practice sports. The term 'active' appears in *On the Genealogy of Morals*, Essay I, for the first time in a specific context in Nietzsche's published works. Nietzsche uses the term 'active' to mean sovereign, strong, spontaneous, pluralistic, and life-affirming, including body-affirming, and opposes it to 'reactive' which is the trait of the millennia-old morality that shaped Occidental values and which is connected to the internalization of instincts or what is called 'repression' in psychoanalysis. An 'active' culture embraces and promotes bodily regimes, including sports.

Foucault's power analytics and the emotions associated with normalizing trends

Foucault on disciplinary power and the panopticon

Foucault accepts the basic teachings of Nietzsche on power, but focuses on their institutional context. Although Foucault does not present a critique of Western institutions of sport, such a critique would have entailed how discursive practices, power relations and truth regimes coincide in the institution of sports in specific historical settings. It is not even clear to me if sports constitute an institution in the limited sense and if such as a critique can be undertaken. Nonetheless, we can try to understand in what ways the disciplinary power of the panopticon permeates sporting practices, as it permeates the whole society, according to Foucault. One area to explore this question is to see how disciplinary bodies are reproduced in sports, in my view, against the spirit of sport. These disciplinary bodies in sports would be the extension of economic and political structures into the sporting arena; for instance, how sports companies have extended and, way more than that, incorporated sporting practices into their marketing fields. Athletes have become marketing symbols; sport fields, their marketing domain. In the domain of politics, Olympic games and other international games have become subject to state or nation-state politics. The control mechanisms and the normalizing trends that Foucault speaks of, especially in *Discipline & Punish*, have become subtler in sports. There are, however, less subtle forms of discipline and control, and this becomes clearer in the cases of Performance Enhancement Drugs (PEDs) and gender issues. An athlete has to prove his or her gender to compete (the selection process is there to establish more or less fair games rather than to set unnecessary limitations on contestants) or the bodies of athletes become arenas of ethical and political debates, subjugated to undue rules and regulations. We then need to understand the kinds of emotions these normalizing trends produce in athletes. Here Foucault's bio-power, his exposition of the workings of disciplinary power and of the way discursive practices, power relations, and truth-telling coincide *on* the body, are revealing and have much to say about body politics in sports and the kinds of emotions they evoke.

Foucault considers our society not one of spectacle, but of surveillance; "under the surface of images, one invests bodies in depth; behind the great abstraction of exchange, there continues the meticulous, concrete training of useful forces . . . the play of signs defines the anchorages of power . . ." (1977: 217). Foucault is here exposing a different paradigm of society, as opposed to those that had considered spectacle or mass media as the defining element of contemporary society. "[I]t is not that the beautiful totality of the individual is amputated, repressed, altered by our social order, it is rather that the individual is carefully fabricated in it, according to a whole technique of forces and bodies" (1977: 217). If we accept Foucault's thesis and if we also consider the sporting field to be a micro-cosmos of society, then we would accept the presence of the panoptic regime and power in sports. That the individual is fabricated means we are not authentic, we are not in touch, or not allowed to be in touch, with our own true emotions (this is even worse for fandom). In the following sections, I will explore this panoptic presence in the several different areas in sports.

Uniformity

One of the effects of the Panopticon is uniformity or homogeneity: "The Panopticon is a marvelous machine which, whatever use one may wish to put it to, produces homogeneous effects of power" (1977: 202). There are not many individual differences left among athletes; clearly athletes in a given field have to play the same sport and under the same rules of that sport, but they can play the same sport with their individual styles and creativity. Such individual coloring exists only minimally. Homogenization of techniques via regulating bodies, the restrictions of teams and their patron corporations, and the demands of fans have created the same type of athlete.

Testing

"[T]he Panopticon was also a laboratory; it could be used as a machine to carry out experiments, to alter behavior, to train or correct individuals. To experiment with medicines and monitor their effects" (1977: 203). Athletes are constantly tested for drugs to see if they are in conformity with established standards; on the other hand, PED producing companies test their new products on them also. They are subjected to different tests for different reasons, but with the same modality of the Panoptic power that aims to classify, discipline, or normalize the athlete under the rules of consumption.

Dismantling the normalizing effects of disciplinary power, which are essentially reactive, which classifies according to categories and regiments, based on docile bodies, and the highly controlling mechanisms of power in sports are challenges to reckon with in the practice of sports. The sporting spirit itself, in my view, is active and operates on an active field; in other words, it does not operate with 'disciplinary power' as Foucault understands and analyzes it and sees it as the main form/exercise of power in our institutions. However, there are extrinsic conditions that may bring reactive elements into sports. These conditions may be social or economic, if not at times political. Many systems of prejudice, corporate money-making demands, hooliganism (raw mass emotions), demands on athletes that they win at any cost (hence the unfair and unilateral use of PEDs), gambling bets, bribes, biased judgments on the part of umpires, abusive trainers and coaches (due to reactive elements they have inherited from their societies), and many others are such reactive elements. Many such practices which do not originate from the culture of sport but are still imposed on it from outside often evoke such deep emotions as hatred, anger, revenge, sadness, and guilt in the members of the sporting community and thereby complicate the already complicated field of emotions.

Emotion and power

Every basic human emotion and its expression can be understood from the standpoint of power and power relations. I would like to approach this subject from two angles: first, from a structural, social standpoint; second, from an individual/existential standpoint.

Structural/social relations: In many socio-cultural settings, emotions are already codified. They have their own power relations and the people who belong to such relations are supposed to feel and express their emotions in certain ways. For instance, in traditional societies one should respect the elderly and never criticize them. Even if one feels anger toward an elder, one is not supposed to show it. The military usually follows a strict rank and file rule and subordinates are supposed to be loyal to their superiors; in these types of power relations, expression of emotion, or even sometimes the feeling of the emotion, is highly restrained. If they are felt, they remain repressed and unexpressed.

Individual/existential perspective: On the other hand, there are loose structures, as among friends for instance or with strangers on the street, where many of the emotional restraints one finds in strict power relations are not present. This is not to say that power relations are entirely absent. We express our anger to exert power against a harm suffered or express jealousy to control our lover or the object of love. Envy is an expression of desire to fill the missing void so as to be powerful in relation to those who already have a desired object. Ambition is a spur to get ahead in power relations. The origin and the affects of these emotions are deeply rooted in the unconscious of the human soul, and the manifestations of their power often remain hidden from those who feel them.

Vertical and horizontal power relations

Every emotion works within specific forms of power relations whether it is power over oneself or power over others. There are horizontal and vertical power relations; players in the same field are in horizontal power relation whereas players and trainers/coaches/umpires are in vertical power relations. And lastly, there are different forms of power in terms of their affects, to follow Nietzsche's distinction, based on whether these affects are life-enhancing or life-denying. The former is 'active,' what could be called a Dionysian (noble) ethics of sporting, and the latter is 'reactive,' an ignoble, sometimes nihilistic, ethics of sporting. If a player blames another player for the defeat of their team because of the latter's mistake, such a player is exercising power over the other. If the blamed figure accepts guilt, then this power exercise becomes effective and 'affective.' A player may commit a foul out of revenge against another player in a different game because of a previous foul committed against him or her. Revenge, in its variegated forms including acts of retribution, is a common power arbiter in human interactions, but is it a meaningful arbiter? Do revengeful acts promote the spirit of sport?

Emotion and value

Human beings are beings that have value, whether such are individual values or socio-cultural ones. Values, often called morals or beliefs (but values are more than them), determine who we are; collective values shape an entire civilization and every age is stamped with such values. We feel emotions according to the values we have or according to what we value; if we have a high self-esteem and someone slights us, we get angry. If we prize material wealth highly, we become envious of those who have such wealth. If retribution is the norm in our culture and a wrongful act is done to us or to someone close to us, we feel vengeful. Values are what human beings create over time; therefore, insofar as emotions are shaped by values, they are subject to socio-cultural, historic conditions. In other words, not every human being would feel anger, envy, and/or revenge under similar circumstances.

It is often forgotten that neither power nor emotion – emotions do have their own power – operates in a vacuum, but rather in and through one's value configuration. While there may be a reciprocal relationship between value and power – one becomes powerful through what is a collective value in a socio-cultural context – we can say that there is a complex relationship between emotion, on the one hand, and value and power, on the other. Although some of our basic emotions may not be entirely value-driven, such as fear of death and danger to life, many others are, as I discussed above. On the other hand, emotions have a complex relationship with power relations. Anger or rage is usually expressed easily in a top to bottom power relation; the coach or trainer screaming at an athlete, for instance. It is often difficult in the reverse direction, depending on the nature of the power relation between the top and the bottom. What I say above, no doubt, depends on the nature of social relations.

If every individual is unique, it is then the task of the trainer/ teacher to bring out that uniqueness in that individual, according to his/her skills, passions, and life goals. Every athlete brings his or her emotional make-up and pathos of power to the sporting community, not only the sporting skills and experience. We are not passive machines where we can isolate one aspect of ourselves from our entire being. We interact with each other closely, especially in sports, and some sports are more physical than others. We work together closely with each other even if we compete against one another; this is what my friend, Emanuel Isidori calls 'co-optition,' a word he coined that connotes both cooperation and competition. The organizers, trainers, coaches, etc., are already there to sustain the spirit of sporting and its power/emotional nature and to pass the torch to new generations. The sporting community must be imbued with positive, uplifting emotions and sustain active forms of power and resist negative emotions and reactive forms of power, which are not autochthonous to sport. The ideal is to create a power of concord between all.

There is an interesting reciprocal relationship between sport and society: on the one hand, society creates the sporting practice; different kinds of sports are created in specific socio-historic settings. On the other hand, sports, while reflecting society itself, can and often do influence social relations. This hermeneutic relationship[1] between the interpreter and the 'interpretans,' or the creator and the creation with its effects, can be elevating if human beings strive and become the best they could be or downgrading if their problems, whether in power relations or emotions, are perpetuated. The hermeneutic relationship can be a vicious circle in which society gets caught up in its lowest common denominator, as we often see in mass sports.

To conclude this chapter, I would highlight the contribution Nietzsche made, following on but expanding further than Spinoza's theory of affect (1989), to culture and thought in the realm of power. Power is rudimentary and works in all levels of our being parallel to the workings of our psychosomatic emotional constitution. Power is expansive, and not identical but rather co-phenomenal to the feelings of pleasure and pain, and hence the necessity of resistance in lateral power relations. One must learn how to resist and fight against hegemonic powers (political in the mega or the micro-sense). Resistance, as it is a form of the expression of power, must also be pleasurable, although oftentimes suffering follows defeat.

In sporting terms, attack and defense would be, respectively, the expansion of and resistance to the sporting power. Finally, in simplistic terms and in terms of its *Gestalt*, power can be active or reactive (this is what we inherited from our past but must be overcome) and both of these *Gestalts* of power have their concomitant emotions. However, there are no words in English or German which stand for these types of emotions. They would be a mixture of emotions already known in current usage; for instance, reactive emotion is a blend of revenge and 'ressentiment.'

Note

1 I have discussed this issue in my essay 'Nietzsche, Sport, and Contemporary Culture' (2017).

Bibliography

Foucault, M. (1977). *Discipline & Punish*. (transl. by A. Sheridan). New York: Vintage Books.

Nietzsche, F. (1982). *Daybreak*. (transl. by R. J. Hollingdale). Cambridge: Cambridge University Press.

———. (1994). *On the Genealogy of Morals*. (transl. by W. Kaufmann). New York: Vintage Press in Basic Writings of Nietzsche edited by W. Kaufmann.

———. (2005). *Thus Spoke Zarathustra*. (transl. by G. Parkes). Oxford: Oxford University Press.

Spinoza, B. (1989). *Ethics*. (transl. by R. H. M. Elwes). Amherst, NY: Prometheus Books.

Tuncel, Y. (2013). *Agon in Nietzsche*. Milwaukee, WI: Marquette University Press.

———. (2017). 'Nietzsche, Sport, and Contemporary Culture'. *Sport, Ethics and Philosophy* 10:4, 349–363.

Chapter 4

Quality of sentiments

Hume is the first thinker to break down the rationalist conception of morality in western thought, although this was already foreseen by Spinoza's theory of affect. With his emphasis on sentiments ('passion' or 'sentiment' are the terms used in his writings), Hume opens the door to examine the nature and quality of human emotions. When he declares that "[M]orality is determined by sentiment. It defines virtue to be *whatever mental action or quality gives to a spectator the pleasing sentiment of approbation*; and vice the contrary," (*EPM* 1998: Appendix 1, ¶10), he points in the direction of exploring emotions that underlie our being and action. What follows is an examination of Hume's ideas as they relate to sport.[1]

Hume highlights such sentiments as sympathy, benevolence, and altruism, all of which he says are needed for morality, social cohesion, and peaceful co-existence. In Book II of *The Treatise of Human Nature*, Hume singles out 'sympathy' as the primary emotion: "No quality of human nature is more remarkable, both in itself and in its consequences, than the propensity we have to sympathize with others, and to receive by communication their inclinations and sentiments" (2000: 206). Here the emphasis is on 'communication,' which enables us to be able to relate to the emotions of others; this is what psychologists call 'empathy.' On the other hand, in *Enquiry*, Hume speaks of 'sympathy' along with 'benevolence' to indicate our capacity to care for others and their sufferings.

Whereas Hume focuses on the object of emotion as its quality (*Treatise* 2000: 184), I emphasize the quality of the emotion and its expression, that is to say, how an emotion is expressed and the nature of its affect (the first one can be more within the control of the expresser than the latter). No doubt, both are related. The origin, the development, the object-attachments, and the affect and affectivity are all related to one another in the making and the expression of emotions.

Between the normative trends regarding basic human emotions propounded by Hume and the egoistic trends of Hobbes, there is a middle ground that has to do with the recognition of our own needs and desires and, at the same time, those of others. It is assumed that there are 'sympathetic' connections in the sporting field; all athletes, whether of the same or an opposing team, are bound by the spirit of sporting and the rules of their game. One often sees sympathetic gestures among the players of opposing teams; for instance, soccer players help each other stand up when they fall.

After Hume, we must ask what types of emotions we need to cultivate collectively and individually. However, we need to go beyond these basic inter-relational emotions and focus on all types of emotions. Here, Nietzsche's reflections would be useful. One finds not only many insights on feelings in Nietzsche's texts, but one also sees a bridge between emotions and quality, and therefore, with esthetics. When I use the term 'quality,' I mean primarily esthetic quality. As Mumford observes in his essay (2012), there are opposing demands of emotions and esthetics. He discusses this theme in relation to a spectator's emotional response and esthetic engagement in sport. For instance, a fan that is emotionally attached to a particular team is unable to appreciate the esthetic qualities of the opposing team. This, of course, is common, but is also reflective of the immaturity of fandom, or any type of fanaticism. While acknowledging the advantage of such emotional attachment on the part of fans, attachment without esthetic qualities, Mumford suggests a way out of this dilemma by proposing to treat emotion as an esthetic category and concludes that these two realms are different and must not be reduced to one another. What needs to be kept in mind here is the quality of the emotion and its expression. The discussion of esthetics pertains not only to beauty, but also to taste. We may be upset when our team is defeated, but to go beyond this emotion and, as spectators, engage in a fight with the opposing team's fan is not only ugly and tactless, but also out of context. When athletes show a similar behavior, this is even worse, because many of their supporters admire them. After all, it is only a game and, as long as a game is played fairly, everyone must accept the defeat and look forward to the next game. The fears of people often translate into such actions, fears that keep them passive in some sense (passive because they are not athletes themselves), but active in entirely meaningless ways when they become fanatics. In short, most people have not dealt with their fears and have not become wholly themselves by turning fears into anxiety, which will open them up to their own authentic selves. This brings us to our next topic.

To play the devil's advocate to Hume – and this critique applies to many classical thinkers – the question of value never comes up in his writings. He speaks of sensations, impressions, reflections, and ideas and perceptions, all of which are some of the basic elements of emotion, but he hardly discusses the question of value. This may be implicit in the notion of 'belief,' but it is not sufficiently presented. For instance, I envy something not only because I sense objects of envy and form an idea of such objects based on how I perceive them, but I envy it because I place value on the object (more often than not, it is a value given by society).

Hume vs. Kant: debate on emotion and rationality in human action/morality[2]

Sentimentalism vs. rationalism

The debate between rationalists and sentimentalists finds its best expression in the philosophies of Kant and Hume, and in the following I will explore some of their ideas. It must be noted that neither of these philosophers created a philosophy of emotion or sentiment per se; rather, their ideas on emotion can be extracted from their moral philosophies to a large extent. That the subject of emotion cannot be confined to morality should be clear from what has been stated often in this book.

Hume, in his *Enquiry*, acknowledges the concurrence of reason and sentiment in almost all moral determinations and conclusions (172), and later, in the same work, explains how, at bottom, human actions are rooted in sentiments and affections: "It appears evident that the ultimate ends of human action can never, in any case, be accounted for by *reason*, but recommend themselves entirely to the sentiments and affections of mankind, without any dependence on the intellectual faculties" (293). Clearly, we should not take Hume's use of these terms for granted and try to understand what he means by them. His use of the terms 'sentiment' and 'affection' overlap with the way 'emotion' is used in this book. By 'reason,' Hume understands that intellectual faculty that discerns, examines causes and effects, and produces principles of science and philosophy (it can be demonstrative and moral); for Hume, reason can be cold and imperfect without the assistance of experience (*Enquiry* 1998: 35–45). Hume traces all human motive and action back to some very basic feelings such as pain and pleasure. Why do we exercise? To remain healthy and to avoid pain. Why do we desire health? Because we desire money, which is pleasurable (*Enquiry* 1998: 293). "[I]t is requisite that there should be some sentiment which it touches, some internal taste or feeling, or whatever you please to call it, which distinguishes moral good and evil, and which embraces the one and rejects the other" (*Enquiry* 1998: 294). Whether Hume is right about pain and pleasure being primordial is one thing; however, he put his finger on the primacy of human sentiments and emotions. And this should count as significant, as well as the fact that he connects sentiments and emotions to the senses, and in this discussion, to taste.

In his moral philosophy, Kant, on the other hand, stands at the opposite end of the spectrum. All emotions must be subordinated to duty and the highest moral law, the Categorical Imperative. To always control emotions and to subject them to a good will with a universal(izing) maxim should be the main goal of every rational being so that he/she acts morally. The good will here is positioned against all inclinations, which include emotions, and all related phenomena, such as passions and affects. The account of affects and passions[3] is presented in Kant's *Anthropology*; because both can damage freedom and self-mastery, they have a negative effect on moral action. In response to sentimentalists, Kant claims in his *Groundwork for Metaphysics of Morals* that: (a) people resort to feelings when they are poor in thinking; (b) feelings cannot supply a measure of good and evil, which means feelings do not contribute to morally right action; and lastly, (c) feelings differ from one another by an infinity of degrees, that is, they are not uniform (1964: 110–111).[4] The first point shows Kant's logo-centric bias toward emotions, which, like the good old Stoics, he believes should always be controlled by reason. The second point attempts to remove or marginalize human emotions and their significance from the economy of human character. Finally, the third point assumes, in a round-about way, that human rationality is uniform across the board, which is far from true, while feelings are variegated. Not only are there different levels of cognition, but there are different forms of thinking along different axes. Kant's emphasis on conscious choice in his moral theory drove him to deny the role of

emotions in human life and character, which are rooted in our psychosomatic functions. Although Kant does not mention Hume here,
he does refer to Hutcheson, the older sentimentalist who established
the moral sense or sentiment to be more important than human reason and whose ideas influenced Hume. However, here we are in the
moral domain, and Kant may argue that what he says on emotions
is relevant insofar as the moral law and the respect for it are concerned; in other words, in his moral philosophy, his main focus was
on emotions that are produced by practical reason (i.e. the feeling
of respect) and not other emotions. What then does the transcendental philosopher, especially one of the third critique, think about
human emotions? This will be our next topic to explore.

According to some Kant scholars, a different Kant emerges in
the *Critique of Judgment* regarding human emotions. Let me state
at the outset that Kant uses a variety of terms, such as *Gefühl*
(feeling), *Empfindung* (no exact word for this exists in English,
but common translation of the word includes sensation, feeling or
emotion), *Affekt*, and *Leidenschaft* (passion), all of which relate,
directly or indirectly, to what we call 'emotion'; and they are all
functions of the field of the sensible (*Sinnlichkeit*) as opposed
to the field of the intelligible. For Angelica Nuzzo, a new transcendental realm of investigation appears in the third critique (in
Cohen 2014: 93), and this has much to do with the unique aspect
of the faculty of Judgment; namely that, unlike Understanding
and Reason, it is not legislative. One question that arises out of
the study of Kant's transcendental philosophy regarding emotions
is whether they play a transcendental role in constituting experience. Is there an emotional experience in and of itself, or are
all emotions simply appendages to cognitive and practical experience? Nuzzo explores these questions based on the relationship
between the emotions and the faculty of judgment as it appears in
Kant's third critique.

In investigating this third critique on the subject of emotion,
Nuzzo states that

> in making room for the power of judgment, its *a priori* prin-
> ciple of purposiveness, and the *a priori* connection with a pecu-
> liar, aesthetic feeling of pleasure and displeasure Kant is in fact
> creating the transcendental space of legitimacy for the emotions
> with the critical discourse.
>
> (in Cohen 2014: 94)

Nuzzo sees a parallelism between the faculty of judgments and the emotions in that they both preside over a subjective realm and are inclusive and overarching in relation to the cognitive and practical domains. She further suggests that judgment reflectively places the subject in touch with her own mental activity and concludes that Kant could have established this renewed position on emotion only in the third critique where he could provide "an integrated transcendental account of the life of the mind as a whole" (in Cohen 2014: 96). Judgment fills up the missing link between Understanding and Reason, as it becomes the connecting faculty; "framed by reflective judgment the emotions can now be allowed in the critical discourse as they gain a sphere of competence of their own *already at the transcendental level*" (In Cohen 2014: 98). Their validity is esthetic: just like esthetic experience, emotional experience is subjective and singular, although it is not a matter of pure subjectivity. As Kant notes, for the way imagination functions in esthetic experience, universality resides in the singular nature of the play of imagination. We can say something similar for emotions, where they are subjective but universal at the same time; however, their universality cannot be understood through the cognitive categories or practical principles. This account of emotions, no doubt, is a radical departure from the 'cold' reason of the first two critiques.

In an attempt to bridge the two positions and to add a few more points, the place from which to understand human emotions cannot be one aspect of human being; all aspects must be considered. Mental, psychic, somatic, and linguistic processes are co-phenomenal, and emotions are grounded in each of them. Rationalism remains at the cognitive, conceptual level and disregards all other aspects and processes that make us human, while sentimentalism could blind us to the dark side of human emotions or could make us naïve in relation to their intricacies and pretensions.

The debate between rationalism and sentimentalism, between those who emphasize human cognitive capabilities and those who focus on human emotions, will not be easily resolved. Let it suffice to say here, despite many insights they may reveal about both, that this debate suffers from mind/body dualism and is unable to approach the human being as a whole, without falling into reductionism. What is more difficult to understand is how human cognition and emotion are interwoven in different individual and socio-cultural contexts. For instance, how does the thinking process work in an individual who acts out of excessive revenge, that is to ask, how does vengeful thinking function? On the other hand, we cannot dismiss the many social, economic, and political reasons for the emotional well-being of human beings, which, no doubt, connects with their overall well-being.

Conclusion to Part I

To understand human emotions and their dynamics, and to see how they help us approach emotions in sport, I explored the ideas of various philosophers and psychologists. On the one hand, the physical, linguistic, or other expression of emotions are forms of discharging our psychosomatic energies. While they occur in all domains of life, in sport, they occur in particular ways. The fundamental question is how we can channel such cathartic expressions. This takes us to the question of the genealogical origin of emotions; here, we need to dive deeper into human character and explain emotions at the level of their rudimentary psychosomatic formation and functioning, hence, the necessity to understand *affects* and *quality* of emotions. These investigations, no doubt, have both macro- and micro-level implications: for the macro-picture, what emotions have currency in a given cultural context? For the micro-picture, what emotions guide or go with the development of individual human beings? Finally, which emotions are sustained or given life to in what power relations? Ultimately, every human society exists in a web of vertical and horizontal power relations that are imbued with emotions, which move from one generational relay to the next with their own transformations.

At the outset, let me state that I disagree with strictly physiological or strictly cognitive accounts of human emotion – these positions suffer from mind/body dualism and concern only one aspect of what or who a human being is. I hold normative claims highly problematic, as they try to establish uniformity out of a diversity of human emotions. There is a place for almost every emotion and its expression, as long as the proper context is established, even for envy and ambition, for instance. These seemingly negative emotions can be channeled to formations where they are externalized without causing any injustice toward others. Normativists' unconscious desire is to efface human diversity, under the name of uniformity. Furthermore, I find such distinctions as 'natural vs. unnatural' emotions highly suspect. For instance, it is suggested that fear is a 'natural' emotion (D'Arms 2005: 16) whereas an emotion like envy is not. In the case of human beings who are endowed with values, it is impossible to assess what is 'natural' and what is 'cultural.' Even if such could be distinguished, emotions of every kind have been 'carved into' civilization for so long that they have become 'natural,' or instinctual. We have made such into instincts. It would take, if not an equally long period, at very least a great length of time to free ourselves of such acculturated emotions. Such would also differ from individual to individual, depending upon their degree of strength, will, determination, physiological composition, etc.

I do not suggest that I have created a complete theoretical framework here; nor was that my aim. However, I believe it has given me sufficient ground to approach and explore many issues that emerge in sport regarding emotions and their expressions.

Notes

1 Despite his stance against the rationalization of sentiments, Hume too suffers from the moralization of human emotions, a trend that goes as far back as Socrates and Plato. Human emotions cannot be confined to the parameters of morality. There are many emotions that have little to do with moral action, right or wrong, not to mention the fact that the deeper strata of emotions, such as affects, do not have a causal relationship to moral action. Therefore, we have to learn how to view emotions in and of themselves. In this regard, I consider the French aphorists (ironically called 'moralists,' which has a different sense than the term 'moral') to be the first 'phenomenologists' of human emotion (phenomenologist in spirit, not method). I did not, could not, benefit from their insights in this book, because it was beyond the scope of my inquiry.

2 Although Hume, like other British philosophers, belongs to the line of passions and sentiments (Descartes could be listed here as well) and Kant belongs to the line of affects (along with Spinoza), these two terms are inter-translatable. Their ideas overlap and explain different dimensions of the same phenomenon.

3 For a taxonomy of emotions (or affective states) in Kant's *Anthropology*, the reader can refer to Deimling's 'Kant's Pragmatic Concept of Emotions' in *Kant on Emotion and Value*, page 110.

4 It is suggested that Kant gave more room for emotions in his early lectures, where he acknowledged the role of moral feelings in moral motivation (Deimling in Cohen 2014: 117).

Bibliography

Cohen, A. (2014). *Kant on Emotion and Value*. New York: Palgrave.

D'Arms, J. (2005). 'Two Arguments for Sentimentalism'. *Philosophical Issues* 15, 1–21.

Hume, D. (1998). *An Enquiry Concerning the Principles of Morals.* (ed. by T. L. Beauchamp). Oxford: Oxford University Press.
———. (2000). *A Treatise of Human Nature.* (ed. by D. F. Norton and M. J. Norton). Oxford: Oxford University Press.
Kant, I. (1964). *Groundwork of the Metaphysics of Morals.* (transl. by H. J. Paton). New York: Harper & Row.
———. (2001). *Critique of Judgment.* (transl. by P. Geyer and E. Matthews). Cambridge: Cambridge University Press.
———. (2011). *Anthropology.* (transl. by R. B. Louden and G. Zöller). Cambridge: Cambridge University Press.
Mumford, S. (2012). 'Emotions and Aesthetics: An Inevitable Trade-Off?' *Journal of the Philosophy of Sport* 39:2, 267–279.

Part II

Sport-specific emotions (SSE)

Having established a theoretical framework in Part I, we now move on to examining sport-specific emotions. First, what do I mean by 'sport-specific'? How can we separate sport-specific emotions from other ones? By 'sport-specific' I mean those emotions that arise due to sport actions and events. There may be a thin line between what is sport-specific and what is not; however, we need to establish a distinction of this sort to be able to understand how certain emotions are felt and invoked more than others in the sporting context. To give some examples: you and your team are faced with a mighty opponent in an international game and fears/anxieties are very high. This is a sport-specific emotion. Your teammate makes a mistake and you are angry; whether justified or not, this is a sport-specific emotion. On the other hand, you are attracted to a player and someone else flirts with the same player and you are jealous; this is not a sport-specific emotion, because the field of sport is not a field of sexuality. Some may argue that one cannot separate sexuality from any human field but I beg to differ. Finally, here is the thin line: some fans hate the fans of the opposing team, not only because they support the opposing team, but also because they belong to a nation they hate. Here two kinds of hatred are mixed: the hate based on the opposing team is sport-specific, but the one based on nationality is not.

What follows in this part is an examination of specific emotions that emerge in sporting contexts, whether they arise directly in the field among players, among fans, between players and referees or coaches, or any combination thereof. I tried to be as comprehensive as possible within the limits of linguistic expression regarding all human emotions. I would have dedicated one chapter to each emotion, but this would have made the book longer and its completion almost impossible.

Chapter 5

Fear, anxiety, pain, suffering, and the question of authenticity

In every human endeavor that involves the unknown, there lurks the possibility of deep emotions such as fear and anxiety. We can speculate that our fears are tied to our self-preservation and that fear of death lies at the root of many of our fears. But a fundamental question remains, which is, what we do with our fears and traumas as we live our lives. Many other deep-seated emotions from love to hate may be tied to fear and its bondage or liberation or transformation.

There is a thin line between fear and anxiety, which are two primary human emotions. I will take a Kierkegaardian line of thinking and suggest that we do not become singular beings unless we overcome our fear and embrace our anxiety.[1] Kierkegaard did not use any examples from the realm/field of sport; being a religious thinker, he took examples from The Bible to illustrate his theory of individualism and authenticity. In his analysis of the story of Abraham and Isaac, Kierkegaard (1981) follows Abraham's emotional journey in the midst of his ordeal with faith; to prove his faith, he agrees to sacrifice his son, Isaac, and in this way he makes what Kierkegaard calls a leap from the ethical (thou shall not kill) to the religious domain (thou shall show thy faith no matter what). These are the last two existential moments in Kierkegaard's thought, the first being the esthetic, which has to do with our everyday lives (the esthetic, the ethical, and the religious are the three moments in this Kierkegaardian hierarchy). What makes Abraham an authentic singular being is the fact that he faced his fear and threw himself into the unknown, into possibilities that he could not foresee. He took the risk of losing his son.

And to extend this line of thinking to Heidegger (1996), we do not become authentic beings unless we deal with our fears and overcome them, as we embrace our anxiety. It is in and through anxiety that we become ourselves. Now, sporting practice, as other practices, opens up a variety of emotions that are normally dormant, such as envy, pride, despair, and anxiety. If channeled in the proper way, the members of the sporting community can mature in these emotions. For instance, to accept defeat and the sadness and humility it can bring about, is a sign of emotional maturity. On the other hand, while scholars such as Jeffrey Fry dismiss hate as a necessary feeling (2003), to hate your opponent in the right dose may in fact be necessary. Fry does not consider the Empedoclean notion of hate or strife (this is not to conflate the two terms, but they are the most common translations of *neikos*), which is the principle that makes individual beings distinct from one another. But to go beyond the necessary dose of such an intense emotion, and beyond the limits of its expression in a particular game, may be ruinous. One can say the same thing for ambition. Athletes must be ambitious, but not over-ambitious. In this context, Fry[2] rightly points to the borderline between the emotion necessary to play a game and when exceeding that proper expression could be harmful for that game. Therefore, the sporting field provides a forum to work on our emotions, especially because it brings them out and intensifies them. It gives every member of the sporting community an opportunity to deal with their fears, such as the fear of defeat, the fear of the unknown, and the fear of death in more risky sports, and channel such fears into anxieties[3] through which they can fulfill their potentiality and become who they are, or become their authentic selves. The major problem with fandom in today's sporting culture is that most people have not had this opportunity to become themselves; we suffer from the dualistic active vs. passive divide, between those who have it and those who do not, which is the case not only in sports but in other socio-cultural arenas as well.

Many athletes in competitive sports encounter the challenge of fear, especially when they face strong opponents in the field. However, if they remain in that moment of fear, it will paralyze them and prevent them from acting. Mohammed Ali tells the story of his fight against Sonny Liston and how he was scared. Despite the odds and the false predictions, and thanks to his transformation of fear into anxiety (i.e. the making of his own self and a great boxer), Ali defeated Liston in the match in 1964, and later in 1965 (Hauser 1997). Similar feelings of fear can appear in athletes who face, individually or as part of a team, stronger, more experienced, and more revered athletes, or 'stars.' In fact, this fear is often used to intimidate the seemingly weaker athlete or team. Those who fall into this trap of intimidation may not perform well, because human beings are not physical machines.

In addition to challenges in the sporting field that could evoke fear and/or anxiety, there are events external to the field that can often lead to trauma. Within the field of sport, traumas can be caused by injuries, pain, near-death experiences, and/or the loss of a teammate or fellow athlete. No doubt, pain is not only a physiological but also a socio-cultural phenomenon; while there is a physical aspect to pain, human beings experience pain based on their beliefs, cultural backgrounds, and perceptions, too. There are, for instance, many social factors in the experience of pain (Loland, Skirstad and Waddington 2006: 18): how is it a lived, embodied, and an emotional experience in addition to being a physical one? Ultimately, each individual experiences, internalizes, and expresses pain differently. There is also a *context* for painful experiences, as for any experience. A small pain for some may be a greater pain for others. This is precisely why we cannot generalize such experiences. Athletes internalize pain in different ways[4] and take it unto themselves during training, actual games, and competitions. Furthermore, the politicization and commercialization of sport contribute to the experience of pain in their own ways. A deeply patriotic athlete, who is under a national gaze due to fame, may feel a deeper pain upon losing at the Olympic games as opposed to another athlete who may not be under similar pressure. Many star athletes and Olympic champions earn money not only through their activities on the field but also from sponsorships and advertisements; any loss of income due to injury can be stressful and trigger depression or trauma. Here we must also add the cost of an injury, especially for athletes who may not be able to cover such costs. There are injuries that put athletes completely out of practice, athletes whose lives are dedicated to and depend on sport. All of these and other reasons can have traumatic effects; without proper remedies, support networks, and immediate interventions, athletes can slide into depression.

Another area where athletes may feel intense fear is in risk or extreme sports (they are also called adventure sports). Although every kind of sport may have its own risks, some have higher degrees of risks not only for injuries but, more significantly, for mortality. Here the fear stems precisely from the greater possibility of dying. Under such sports, we can count some of the winter sports such as rock climbing, most of the board sports (such as surfing and bodyboarding), combat sports, horse races, and auto racing. There have been debates as to whether such risk sports are consistent with the idea of the good life. Let me state, first of all, that there is no one good life for everyone; second, such risk-taking can be construed as one's good life, as McNamee observes at the end of his introduction to *Philosophy, Risk and Adventure Sports* (2007). In the spirit of Kierkegaard, McNamee upholds that risk-taking can open up new vistas for individuals so that they can transform themselves. Without the risk, we would be in stagnation; some may prefer a complacent life, but not everyone does. And sport itself is not a life of stagnation, but rather of growth and frequent transformation.

On the other hand, what stands in opposition to risk may be safety and not stagnation, and this is the primary concern in everyday human life, as Breivik mentions (in McNamee 2007: 11). Zigzagging between the homogeneous and the heterogeneous of Bataille's registers for human life and skiing through the unchartered territory of Heidegger's being-toward-death, Breivik accepts the ethos of risk-taking in sport as he writes: "there are many good reasons to give support to a more risk accepting attitude" (in McNamee 2007: 12). As he presents both sides in this debate, he makes a good case for risk-taking. First, risk-taking prepares us for the unknown and the uncertain; after all, human life is full of uncertainty. When we take risks, we do not know the outcome; we can try to control it, but we cannot know it fully; otherwise, it would not be risky. Second, through risk-taking we can deal with the "beast within" (16); this dealing with the beast within is what Nietzsche calls 'transfiguration,' which is related to 'sublimation' in Freud (the latter may be a more tamed version of the former). Third, the evolutionary process shows that human beings have taken risks all along – risk-taking is part of our genetic make-up (17). Finally, risk-taking makes us stronger, which is why Breivik advises that children be raised to experience difficulties in life like heat, cold, and hunger (20). With these remarks, Breivik approaches one of Nietzsche's fundamental teachings, to strive and aim for strength rather than weakness, which is one aspect of Nietzsche's conception of the Overhuman. Excitements, thrills, and sensationalism are, in my view, side phenomena; the crux of risk-taking lies in the points made in the preceding text, and also in what Heidegger calls being-toward-death. This returns us to Breivik's analysis of skydiving.

Breivik analyses skydiving from the standpoint of Heidegger's philosophy, as he focuses on authenticity. What he says about skydiving, which is that it opens Dasein (Being) up to a possibility of death and from there on to an authentic way of living, applies to every sport. Although skydiving may be riskier than most other sports, athletes often face issues of anxiety and authenticity in different types of sport. On the other hand, the notion of death should not be taken in the sense of a physical death; an athlete may 'die' when he or she loses a match. In the spirit of Kierkegaard and Heidegger, Breivik explains the relationship between fear and anxiety in the act of skydiving:

> From a Heideggerian perspective the situation after the exit from the airplane where one falls through the void, filled with anxiety, is the original situation. It reveals the naked human condition in the world. A specific phobia, like the fear of heights or fear of flying, is a specific modification of anxiety into a fear that one can handle by taking precautions and making oneself safe in various ways. Anxiety is usually considered as something negative that should be avoided or treated, but for Heidegger it is an important and necessary condition for getting to know the deepest aspects of human existence. Anxiety reveals that ultimately we are finite beings that have to relate in one way or other to our own death. For Heidegger being-toward-death is not related to the biological phenomenon of passing away as a physical being. Nor is it the simple event of one's life being over, as it is sooner or later over for everyone. Instead, death is Dasein's own last and definite possibility. It is the possibility of impossibility. It gives Dasein's life a wholeness and totality. Death is something inside one's life that one always has to relate to, either by covering it up or by facing its reality.
> (Breivik 2010: 38)

Furthermore, Breivik makes a distinction between two types of anxiety, namely between a structural one and a motivational one: the former has to do with Dasein's tendency

> to fall into the world and understand itself from the perspective of a world of things. This absorption in the world is a necessary part of the human being-in-the-world. From this perspective

both inauthentic and authentic living have the same 'value' because they are necessary parts of the ways Dasein exists.

(2010: 40)

On the other hand, in the motivational account, "Dasein flees from the nullity experienced in the face of anxiety" (2010: 40). While the former is descriptive, the latter has the undertones of an existential imperative. Both perspectives expose the nature of anxiety, especially in relation to fear, and show what can be done about it so as to achieve authenticity. Breivik's study of skydiving emphasizes the phenomenon of void and the possibility of a total disappearance of that world into void, which can be summed up as 'being-toward-death.' This is not death itself, but a constant reminder of our mortality: "We are thrown into the world and our exit from it is deadly. Risk sport reminds us of this in a very concrete way" (Breivik 2010: 40). Finally, Breivik brings up Russell's approach to risk sports, which emphasizes self-affirmation and the potential to test limits and press beyond (2005: 14). In everyday life we rarely have the chance to test our limits, because we are burdened by the chores of everyday reality. Sport, especially risk sports, create such a chance. This issue of limits and going beyond the limits is explored both by Bataille and Blanchot in their works on ecstasy and limit experience (1985 and 1992, respectively), though not in a sporting context.

Finally, and related to the previous discussion, Ilundain takes a look at the sublime by way of Kant and relates it to the experience of limits, the joy of overcoming limits, and ultimately mortality. Awe in the face of magnanimity and those that are grand underlies the

mathematically sublime which . . . enables us to go from the finite to the infinite, from the limited to the limitless. In the case of the extreme, the limits being overcome are those of perception and of what we think is physically possible.

(in McNamee 2007: 155)

Ilundain moves on to show how skateboarding illustrates such extremes and the joy a skateboarder may feel at the conquest of seemingly impossible moves. In agreement with Breivik and Russell, Ilundain presents a deep insight into human emotions: "The extreme is a wonderful way to enrich and concurrently experience some of the most complex yet basic emotions proper to life, and in intensities that are barred from our mundane lives" (in McNamee 2007: 160). This is not to say that Ilundain would endorse every intense emotion for the sake of its intensity; there is a context here, which is that of the sublime in sport. And I do not think the intensity is meant for every type of emotion in a sporting context.

Ultimately, all of these issues, fear-anxiety, all fear-related phenomena such as horror, awe, terror, and trauma, limit experiences, testing, and going beyond limits, the finite and infinitude, mortality, and immortality, bring us to the subject of the Dionysian, as Nietzsche presented it in his first published book, *The Birth of Tragedy*. The Dionysian means the absence of the individuated state, or the Apollonian, which translates as our mortality. However, the Dionysian truth is harsh to face and can paralyze or drag us into despair, if we were to be obsessed with it; this is why pleasurable illusions are needed, illusions that also coincide with action, through which we can embrace life and affirm it in its full span. Nietzsche saw this interaction in Greek tragedy (1967), but, to the dismay of many scholars who dismiss contemporary sport as mass entertainment, such interaction also exists in sport, a field where creative and destructive forces meet head-on, in fact, more so, more forcefully and viscerally than in Greek dramatic performance. In his later works, Nietzsche brought these two forces together into one thought, the eternal return of the same. Sport is the living reality of the eternal return of the same, of cyclical games, where athletes die and are re-born, whether in small or big ways, whether in defeat or victory.

In what ways can we discharge the emotion of fear? Some fear will always remain, even if we deal with our fears and transform them into authentic being-making anxieties, and it will be different sorts and intensities of fear, depending upon our character. The question here is how a catharsis can be affected in a sporting context. Discharge should not mean simply externalization, but also the conquering and transformation of fear, or whatever emotion; in sport, one can conquer the fear of loss and defeat and become victorious (and in that to even learn how to deal with the feeling of victory). One can also conquer the fear of performance (which may be the case for initiates), what is often called 'performance anxiety.'

What are the affects that lie at the root of fear and anxiety? A sense of being overwhelmed in the face of larger forces that cannot be controlled, the unknown nature of these forces, and feeling small, weak, and helpless may all contribute to our fears. The affect of fear is real; however strong one may be, one remains very small in the face of every other cosmic and natural force, yet, one has to be strong to live or, at least, make-believe in one's strength. How we can achieve this balance, how to understand the affects that operate in us in mysterious ways, remains a challenge.

How do fear and anxiety come into play in power relations? Fear, like many other emotions, has had its place in the evolution of the human species and its survival; it is a primary human emotion. Despite its role for self-preservation, it can also paralyze and inhibit the individual and can prevent, and often does, the individual from realizing his/her full potential. The fear of death and of the unknown, the uncertain, and the unexpected often lie on the path of every human being. On the other hand, existing social structures reinforce these fears so that the rulers can subjugate their subjects with ease and forestall rebellion (Machiavelli's advice for rulers exemplifies this fact). In addition to existential fears, individuals are faced with fears imposed on them by their society. Fears then become embedded in the very social fabric and in its power relations. To be ourselves, to be authentic, we need to be able to turn some of those fears into anxieties so as to open up new possibilities for transformation, as in sport, which is one such field of possibilities.

Where do our fears and anxieties stem from? Are they entirely irrational and to be cast aside as such? We are all mortal beings and most of our fears ultimately stem from our mortality and all related phenomena such as loss; in sport, this is often experienced as the loss of life, injury, or defeat, all of which are associated with pain and suffering. For a long time, emotions have been dismissed either as irrational or subjective by almost every philosopher from Plato to Kant. McNamee refutes both positions. Regarding the irrationality of emotions, he states that, in an emotional moment, athletes are responding "in part to a judgment or an interpretation of their situation" from which much can be learned.

> Moreover, the emotions can be allowed a much more positive role in our identification of what matters to us in both fleeting and more considered ways. While it is easy to recall instances when emotions have got in the way of good judgment, or indeed been obstacles to right action, we can also think of examples where our emotional (though still cognitively based) responses are salient.
> (McNamee in Loland, Skirstad, and Waddington 2006: 231)

While I agree with McNamme, I would also add that emotions and thought are often so fused together that we cannot separate one from the other. Thinking can exist even in the angriest outburst. In other words, cognition is not free from its emotive component, and vice versa. What McNamee highlights here is the fact that emotions should not be seen only in a negative light; they have a positive role in human life and interactions, which can be approached in multiple ways. This, no doubt, has to do with the quality of emotions and their *affective* dimension. As for the subjectivity of emotions, we should try to understand what is meant by subjectivity: first, it can mean that the subject is constitutive (in a Cartesian sense) of all his/her actions; this means that the subject is in total control of their emotions. This is far from being true because, more often than not, we are not in control of our emotions (let's also keep in mind that what is felt and what is expressed are not the same). Second, meaning, which is more of common parlance, is that emotion is unique to the individual who feels it. However, emotions are felt individually, the fact that they have collective dimension has been amply demonstrated in this book (for instance, see the part on affect theory); these two positions are not mutually exclusive. A specific emotion may have common acceptance in a cultural context, and individuals may feel that emotion because of that. Moreover, McNamee adds two counter-arguments against the subjectivity of emotions: first, emotions entail judgments; second, emotions are influenced by space and time (McNamee in Loland, Skirstad, and Waddington 2006: 231).

Pain and suffering

Pain and suffering are inevitable in human life,[5] but do we need more of them simply by creating practices, like sport, where we suffer more and where, in some sports, we inflict suffering on others intentionally or unintentionally? Why do human beings desire to be active rather than inactive? Before I examine these questions, I would like to say a few things on the pain/suffering distinction. Suffering, and all its related phenomena, is a human condition that is associated with loss or lack and is often seen as undesirable – I say this tentatively, because what is desirable is not always known and sometimes suffering itself may be desired – and manifests itself in different forms as in anguish (mental suffering) or pain (physical suffering). Distinctions among these different types of sufferings are hard to establish from an integral approach and I agree with McNamee's skepticism (McNamee in Loland, Skirstad, and Waddington 2006: 232–234). Regarding the separation of suffering from pain or vice versa, McNamee ties it to mind/body dualism that was prevalent in Western thought since Descartes. Even if we can separate suffering and pain from one another heuristically, their relationship remains to be as complex as the body/mind relationship. To complicate the subject further, there are cultural and individual factors that play a role in the way we suffer and feel pain. McNamee then examines positions in medical ethics (234–236). Sticking to the dualism between pain and suffering, at least for heuristic purposes, it can be said that there is a causal relationship between the two. This position is hard to maintain, because it would mean that a specific type of pain would cause the same type of suffering in every person who feels that pain. On the other hand, not every pain leads to suffering. The subject becomes more complicated when it comes to understanding whether a person is suffering or not; is suffering entirely a private affair? If, like a true Stoic, the sufferer shows no signs of their suffering/pain, yes; but, more often than not, sufferers, especially when the suffering/pain is intense, do show signs, whether physical or linguistic. If this occurs in the public arena, as in sporting events, then they are no longer the private affairs of athletes, but they become *affects* shared by the sporting community in different ways and degrees. Finally, on suffering and consciousness, can one suffer without being conscious of one's suffering? McNamee thinks not:

> However, although one may be injured without being in pain, one cannot be said to suffer without the cognitive aspect of the emotion registered at some conscious level. This condition seems indisputable for human suffering. Put formally, we might say that it is the awareness of some seriously negative happening – is a necessary condition of suffering but not a sufficient one.
>
> (McNamee in Loland, Skirstad, and Waddington 2006: 235)

Although McNamee's context and example is sport, what he concludes is far from true. Humans do suffer without being aware of their suffering, as with cases of trauma, for instance. This is one of the fundamental problems of human existence, that we do suffer from things unknown to us; the origin of suffering remains unconscious, but shows itself in its symptoms. McNamee would counteract that he is speaking of pain, but pain and suffering are integral and cannot be easily separated. Therefore, one can suffer[6] without it being registered at the level of consciousness.

I now want to return to the question I posed above: why do we seek activities like sports, which bring about pain and suffering, while we can remain passive? Are we sado-masochistic? Is sport a sado-masochistic field? This question is posed by Jim Parry in his essay 'The Intentional Infliction of Pain in Sport: Ethical Perspectives.' After examining various forms of pain from discomfort to harm and hurt, Parry examines intentional inflictions of pain in sport, especially those that are caused by intra-contest violence. In order to do this, he distinguishes between assertion, aggression, and violence (Parry in Loland, Skirstad and Waddington 2006: 147). As Parry observes, many forms of pain infliction are intrinsic to sport; however, the context in which such inflictions are done and how they are done should be kept in mind. It is not sufficient to emphasize intention while dismissing acts and omissions for which athletes should be held responsible. With these remarks, Parry emphasizes the context in which the infliction of pain happens. Another distinction Parry brings to light is the one between violent acts and acts of violence, and similarly, aggressive acts and acts of aggression. The latter are determined by the consequences of actions. In other words, the goal of acts of violence is precisely to inflict harm and pain, and, if I understand him correctly, such acts should not be permitted in sports, because they do not fit with the spirit of sporting. I agree with Parry's conclusion that sport is not a sado-masochist act, not because of his first reason, that sport is 'not a sexual perversion,' but rather because of his second, that "in sport we are not taking pleasure in the pain itself, or in cruelty for its own sake. The pain is instrumental: no pain, no gain" (Parry in Loland, Skirstad, and Waddington 2006: 161). Pain is a sign, an indicator, and even a motivator.

In conclusion, most human fear stems from mortality, limitation, and/or the unknown. Those who have surrendered themselves to a supernatural being and its design may not feel fear because they see their lives as part of destiny (as do the Stoics, for instance), but this does not mean that they have really dealt with fear; they simply cloaked it with veils of illusion. Sporting, however, does not involve such forms of surrender; it is an active field, it is a field of not accepting one's given destiny, but rather of making one's self and, as such, it is wrought with the primary human emotions of fear, despair, sadness, joy, anxiety, and suffering. It is a field where one could become who one is, where one could re-fashion a life for one's self, but it has to be done while such primary emotions are also worked out and worked up to higher realms.

Notes

1 It is important to keep in mind that so-called existentialist thinkers such as Kierkegaard and Heidegger use the term 'Angst' (translated as 'anxiety') differently than the way it is used in most psychological literature.
2 My disagreement with Fry lies in where the line is drawn. He is more cautious than me about accepting 'hate' in sports.
3 One good example of this type of transfiguration of fear into anxiety is from Norwegian athletes and their activities and achievements in high-risk winter sports.
4 There have been many debates in the medical community about boxing and its short- and long-term injurious effects on boxers. This topic was explored by Ken Sheard in 'Pain and Injury in Boxing' in the anthology edited by Loland (2006). As Sheard shows, the medical community is split on this subject, but the more important question is why it is the medical establishment, or any other not related to sport or boxing, that makes an ethical decision on a sporting subject. Furthermore, from a philosophical standpoint, one could argue that the infliction of harm has its own place in culture and cultural activities, including sports, and would be ethically sound as long as it has a context, has levels (weight levels in boxing), and happens among more or less equals. The unintentional harm inflicted in many other fields of sport must be considered if one wishes to address this question with any degree of equity.
5 I argued for this position in my essay published in the anthology *Nietzsche and Transhumanism* and showed how the desire to eliminate all pain and suffering lacks an understanding of deeper human emotions. Such desire is propelled by utopianism, which, philosophically, is bankrupt. It is rooted in a linear conception of time which neglects the cyclical and repetitive nature of all that is, as formulated in Nietzsche's idea of the eternal return of the same, and in other philosophers' conceptions of time. Self-knowledge of who we are must be closely bound by our strife to evolve and to excel. All sport practice also supports this fundamental philosophical wisdom.
6 Suffering here is only thought of in one way. To be passionate is also a form of suffering; so, anyone who wishes to live a passionate existence has to be willing to suffer. There is no passion without suffering. The very word passion comes from the Late Latin *passionem* (nominative *passio*) 'suffering, enduring' from past participle stem of Latin *pati* 'to endure, undergo, experience' a word of uncertain origin. The meaning strong emotion, desire is late 14th century, from Latin's render of the Greek *pathos*. One can think too of the suffering one often endures when training as an athlete, which is often not pleasant, a necessary form of suffering to reach higher degrees of self-mastery.

Bibliography

Bataille, G. (1985). *Visions of Excess.* (transl. by A. Stoekl). Minneapolis, MN: University of Minnesota Press.

Blanchot, M. (1992). *The Infinite Conversation.* (transl. by S. Hanson). Minneapolis, MN: University of Minnesota Press.

Breivik, G. (2010). 'Being-in-the-Void: A Heideggerian Analysis of Skydiving'. *Journal of the Philosophy of Sport* 37:1, 29–46.

Fry, J. P. (2003). 'On Playing with Emotion'. *Journal of the Philosophy of Sport* 30:1, 26–36.

Hauser, T. (1997). *Muhammad Ali in Perspective.* San Francisco, CA: Collins.

Heidegger, M. (1996). *Being and Time.* (transl. by J. Stambaugh). Albany, NY: SUNY Press.

Kierkegaard, S. (1981). *The Concept of Anxiety.* (transl. by R. Thomte). Princeton: Princeton University Press.

Loland, S., Skirstad, B. and Waddington, I. (2006). *Pain and Injury in Sport: Social and Ethical Analysis.* New York: Routledge.

McNamee, M. (2007). *Philosophy, Risk, and Adventure Sports.* London: Routledge.

———. (2008). *Sports, Virtues and Vices.* London: Routledge.

Nietzsche, F. (1967). *The Birth of Tragedy.* (transl. by W. Kaufmann). New York: Vintage Press.

Parry, J. (2006). 'The Intentional Infliction of Pain in Sport: Ethical Perspectives'. In S. Loland, B. Skirstad and I. Waddington (eds.), *Pain and Injury in Sport: Social and Ethical Analysis.* New York: Routledge.

Russell, J. S. (2005). 'The Value of Dangerous Sport'. *Journal of the Philosophy of Sport* 32, 1–19.

Sheard, K. (2006). 'Pain and Injury in Boxing'. In S. Loland, B. Skirstad and I. Waddington (eds.), *Pain and Injury in Sport: Social and Ethical Analysis.* New York: Routledge.

Tuncel, Y. (2017). 'Pain and Suffering in Nietzsche and Transhumanism'. In Y. Tuncel (ed.), *Nietzsche and Transhumanism* (pp. 220–230). New Castle upon Tyne, UK: Cambridge Scholars Publishing.

Chapter 6

Other specific feelings in sporting context

Anger, depression (or despair), envy, guilt, sadness et al.

Anger

Anger is an emotional response to a suffered injury or injustice. Aristotle defines anger as "a desire accompanied by pain for an imagined retribution on account of an imagined slighting inflicted by people who have no legitimate reason to slight oneself or one's own" (1994: 1378a31–33). Nussbaum analyzes Aristotle's definition and highlights the fact that anger is a complex emotion spanning between pain and pleasure; the injury inflicts pain and the imagined retribution gives pleasure (2016: 17). There are several issues in the phenomenon of anger: (a) it is subjective: the person feels anger (both the injury and retribution) in his or her own particular way; (b) the target of anger is typically a person (17); (c) the one who instigates the anger may be completely ignorant of the anger he or she has caused (18); and (d) what creates the anger may have to do with that person's being, value, title, status, belonging, etc. In honor culture, for instance, down-ranking causes much anger.

Common causes of anger in sport

Intentional or seemingly intentional or accidental fouls (if there is a severe injury, this may intensify the anger). Interference by referees at the right moment for the right reasons would alleviate any excessive anger. With our advanced technological age, it is now possible to see such fouls from close-up; and technology can help referees to make the best possible decision at the right time. Most fouls evoke anger in the athlete to whom the foul is done; intentional, vicious, and the most damaging fouls would provoke the greatest anger.

Misjudgment on the part of referee(s). Assuming that referees are always fair, human error and/or misjudgment still remain possible. It is understandable that athletes get angry when they are unjustly penalized. With the help of advanced technology (zoom-in cameras and instantaneous coordination with the on-field referee), such errors can be minimalized.

Mistakes made by teammates (anger increases if they are avoidable mistakes). One often sees soccer players shaking their hands or heads in signs of anger, because while they were skipped their chosen teammate could not score a goal. Sometimes you see players screaming at their teammates for making mistakes or blaming teammates for defeat.

Poor performance (this may invoke the wrath of the coach). Performance depends upon a variety of factors, one of which includes being in good mood, to be in a high-energy state. Another factor concerns condition and stamina. It is often forgotten that energy is finite. Even if athletes who train well have more energy than non-athletes, they still have finite energies. Anyone who reaches the limits of his/her energy clearly cannot perform well. If a coach is unable to read clues about energy, the athlete cannot but simply maintain a poor performance for which he or she cannot be blamed. In other words, because an athlete is so immersed in a game, he or she doesn't have the ability to be as self-aware about energy, mood, etc., and it is the duty of the coach to discern any shift in mood and energies. The coach can help regulate the athlete toward optimal effects.

Awful climate and bad field conditions. Such conditions often make it more difficult, if not even dangerous for athletes to play. In such cases, it would be best to cancel games, but this is often not done due to logistic reasons and tight schedules. There are ordeals and challenges in sport and athletes are competing in similar harsh conditions, but they are not necessarily trained to compete in such conditions.

Fandom and fan attitude toward the rival team. Fans are an undifferentiated group of people whose main function is loyalty to their team; they come from a variety of backgrounds and may not even be interested in the spirit of sport. Or, they zealotry could blind them to it. The out-of-context behavior of fans often complicates the sporting field, causing much anger in the fans of the opposing team. Loyalty and zealotry are not the same things, but many sport fans do not separate them in the heat of the game. One example for this type of anger is Eric Cantona's reaction to a fan at the football game of Manchester United against the home team Crystal Palace, played in London's Selhurst Park on January 25, 1995. Cantona who, according to his own version, was being irritated all throughout the game by Richard Shaw, was sent off for kicking out against him. As Cantona was walking out of the field toward the dressing-room, a Crystal Palace supporter moved down to the front of the crowd and threw xenophobic expletives at Cantona, all of which had to do with his being French. In response, Cantona gave a kung-fu kick to the fan (The Guardian, January 25, 1995).

Psychological studies have shown that aggression toward athletes often causes anger, but it would be more precise to speak of 'undue aggression,' because there are acts of aggression that are acceptable in sport. Stressful encounters, the proximity to goal-making, performance level, and anger-rumination are also factors that contribute to anger (Sofia and Cruz 2016), not to mention provocations by fans and other causes that do not originate from sport practice.

Expressing one's anger is often cathartic; one discharges the emotion/affect and this has a place in our psychic life. We must, however, investigate the origin and the affect of anger and try to understand in what sport contexts it may be acceptable or unacceptable. Clearly, no one can control how emotions are felt and expressed because every human being feels and expresses emotions according to his or her own emotional constitution. Notwithstanding such, managers, coaches, trainers, and referees have a great role to play in the total emotional experience of the games played.

Antidote to anger: first, it is best not to create the conditions that would invoke anger whatever our position may be in the sporting community. On the other hand, athletes have to develop coping mechanisms (what is called 'anger management' in this context) and learn how to remain calm and refrain from actions that would damage their own reputation, team, or opponents, and, more importantly, the spirit of sport and playing fairly.

Depression and despair

Despair is an emotional state in which there is no hope and it often arises when there is a great discrepancy between what one is or where one is and the goal one sets for oneself to achieve. Despair is not only a sign of hopelessness, but more often than not, a sign of powerlessness. Sartre lists 'despair' as one of the three fundamental human emotions to reckon with, along with 'anxiety' and 'abandonment' (Sartre 2007). Despair may be the collective effect of the nihilism of our age, as diagnosed by Nietzsche and Russian thinkers such as Turgenev and Dostoyevsky. If there is no meaning in life, then why live and act at all? Sartre's Nietzschean dictum is to create your own meaning and have your own hope and to set your own standards to excel so that you feel first nothing in relation to them and then find your authenticity in attaining those goals. Sport is one such area of meaning and meaning-creation in which we find our own nascent freedoms.

It is beneficial to make a distinction between episodic despair and chronic despair. In the former, one feels hopelessness in the face of overwhelming circumstances, a stronger opponent, for instance, or when facing seemingly negative events. "No matter what, I or we will not be able to perform well or win" may be an underlying motive and expression for despair. Although one can fall into despair, one can emerge from it and not remain in that state. In contrast, despair becomes chronic if one cannot free oneself of it. One can then sink into further despair and its dismal landscape. No hope, no end of the tunnel is seen. Many depressions, suicides, or suicide attempts[1] often stem from chronic forms of despair. Despair can root in the core of one's being and alter? what one shall become. In sport, despair can originate from loss (of any kind), defeat, lack of needed support, mistreatment (by anyone), abuse, injury (especially severe injuries that impede athletes from playing), misjudgment on the part of a referee during a game, and out of context attempts to win a game by some athletes (doping, game-fixing, etc.).

One good example from recent sport history for turning potential despair into hope is the victory of the US men's Olympic hockey team formed out of mostly amateurs and college players against the all time victorious Soviet hockey team of some of the best and experienced players at the 1980 Winter Olympics in Lake Placid. The Soviets had dominated the field for the last 20 years. Team USA won the game 4–3, setting an example for those who struggle and never lose hope. (Wikipedia: 'Ice hockey at the 1980 Winter Olympics').

Antidote to Chronic Despair: athletes must know, more or less, the level of their skills and what they can and cannot do in their own fields. Such self-knowledge emerges during practice and actual games. Furthermore, athletes must accept their skill level without falling into complacency and without ceding the idea to excel. However, one can only excel incrementally. On the other hand, athletes need to learn how to accept defeat and how to turn it to an advantage[2] for future games. After all, sport is a perpetual, playful process, with ups and downs, victories, and defeats, along the way. All of them must be seen as part of that process. Defeat is difficult to accept, but transforming it into a scheme of empowerment may be sweeter than a short victory, as I argued in my essay "Defeat, Loss, Death, and Sacrifice in Sport" (Tuncel 2015).

Envy

Envy is often considered to be a 'negative' emotion; it is seen as spiteful and reactive. Envy is underlain by the desire to possess something one does not have; it is the feeling of lack that informs the desire to possess. It defines the relationship between the haves and the have-nots, understood in the widest sense, not only in terms of money and wealth. It can propel the envier to obtain the missing object of desire, sometimes at any cost, and the envier may want the object only for him or herself. Envy is largely seen in this negative light probably because of such spitefulness. However, one can envy loftier goals and heights and may not want to preclude others from such goals. In this sense, it functions, like ambition, as a positive force, an emotion that pushes us forward and upward.

Nietzsche explains these two different types of envies by way of ancient Greece and its goddess Eris. Borrowing from Hesiod's *Works and Days*, he distinguishes between two forms of envy as part of his concept of agon. The good Eris inspires human beings to higher goals through competitive fights (as in contests) while the bad Eris provokes them to engage in annihilatory fights (as in wars).

> And not only Aristotle but the whole of Greek antiquity thinks differently from us about hatred and envy, and judges with Hesiod, who in one place calls one Eris evil, namely, the one that leads men into hostile fights of annihilation against one another, while praising another Eris as good, the one that, as jealousy, hatred, and envy, spurs men to activity: not to the activity of fights of annihilation, but to the activity of fights of contest.
>
> (Nietzsche 1976: 35)

Following this observation, Nietzsche claims that the way we conceive of envy separates us from the ancient Greek world: "The Greek is envious and does not consider this quality a blemish but the gift of a benevolent godhead: what a gulf of ethical judgment lies between him and us!" (1976: 35).

Goldie too discusses envy, from a psychological standpoint, and asks the question as to whether envy is a vice. He rightly takes note of the different types of envy. He mentions harmless and harmful envy. "If the envy is of the non-malicious type, general sort, it can be quite harmless so far the envied person is concerned, and can be an effective spur for the envious person" (2003: Chapters 8, 3–4). On the other hand, he suggests that envy is often of a malicious sort. By way of Gabrielle Taylor's definition of envy as the emotion of "other-directed hostility and destruction," Goldie relates it to self-esteem: "the good that is envied is wanted not necessarily for its own sake, but also for the sake of improving the envious person's self-esteem" (2003: Chapters 8, 3–4). These are all too common forms of envy many human beings feel, and Goldie acknowledges this view of emotions when he refers to them as 'facts of nature.' Although much of what he writes is revealing about envy, he too falls short of considering 'positive envy' or the other kind of envy (desiring what one does not have) that propels people to higher goals, and in sports to higher levels of performance and victory. This could be due to the fact that Goldie is speaking of this human condition in a general way or that he is not concerned with agonistic strife, which can be utilized to create a higher self in and through contest (as in competitive sports). It must also be noted here that the main subject of this chapter is jealousy. To his credit, he does say envy need not be like this, meaning not only of the malicious kind: "so it does not follow that envy is necessarily a vice. Indeed, it can be a virtue" (2003: Chapters 8, 5). How and why envy is a virtue is not discussed though; it is postponed to the end of the chapter.

In a sporting context, envy could occur when athletes yearn for better performance, more goal-scoring, star players, highest medals, and, if defeated in a game, for the victor. Some philosophers call this emotion 'emulation' and distinguish it from envy. Hobbes reserves the latter for anything that is spiteful:

Emulation is grief arising from seeing oneself exceeded or excelled by his concurrent, together with hope to equal or exceed him in time to come, by his own ability. But, envy is the same grief joined with pleasure conceived in the imagination of some ill fortune that may befall him.

(1969: Volume 1, 9)

Emulation is associated with rivalry and is a form of envy that stems from it; it is the envy of the winner and what comes with being a winner. No doubt, all such emotions, including *Schadenfreude*, spite, and resentment, are adjacent emotions in the economy of the human psyche, but we cannot relegate every form of envy to the lower level of negativity, the way philosophers and theologians have done for several millennia.

Human beings have developed different attitudes or emotional dispositions to deal with a deeply rooted emotion such as envy. Herzog (2000) explores many which are applicable to the sporting context, some of which I will examine here: (a) preempting the rise of envy by removing its condition. Herzog gives the example of what Achilles does in the funeral games for Patroclus (149) – Achilles honors Agamemnon before he can even show his superior skill in archery; (b) one can remove or destroy the object of envy (Herzog 2000: 149); in sport an underdog can defeat a star or a star team; (c) one can take joy in the suffering of the object of envy (149); this connects envy to *Schadenfreude*; and (d) one can downgrade the value of the object of envy (150), what is often called 'sour grapes'; for instance, in sport, one can downgrade the importance of a game and its end-result when the winner is an excellent team or athlete. Related to this, one can also find blemishes in the object of envy so as to render it non-enviable.

Herzog refers to emulation, *Schadenfreude*, and spite as "possible responses to envy, not partly constitutive of envy itself" (153). But how can we separate responses from constitutive elements in the field of affects? This remains an open question. What propels me to envy specific objects (response to envy) is not too distinct from what makes me envious in general (constitutive elements) in the psychosomatic domain. In other words, emotions do not follow the rigid rules of causation; if that were the case, we would all feel the *same* emotion in the *same* context and for the *same* object.

One possible antidote to spiteful envy is to replace it with uplifting envy, envy not for false, mundane, entirely egoistic goals, but rather for higher goals for oneself and others – while self-interested, we also co-exist with others, and both altruism and egoism are emotionally deficient states. In short, replace the bad Eris with the good Eris to use Nietzsche's recasting of Hesiod's phrases (1976: 35). Understanding every emotion that is in us reflects some of our character traits. Envy in its different degrees and expressions shows what we value most and how we live up to it and strive to achieve it. Some objects, and some envies, are not as valuable as others. On the other hand, without envy (and ambition) for higher goals and achievements and exemplary models, there would not be much strife and contest.

Guilt (and blame)

Blaming others, finding guilt when there is a problem, is a common human trait. It is one thing when it happens in family or in relationships, but something altogether different in other contexts; on a grander scale, its impact can be devastating (as in genocides and ethnic cleansings). Athletes and coaches are not exceptions; blaming some athletes for defeat, whether it comes from a fellow teammate or coaches and managers, happens frequently and its emotional cost on the blamed one is heavy. In the field of sport, we see players screaming, shaking their heads, or making expressive hand gestures, sometimes ones considered vulgar. Blaming is common, but where is its seed/origin? And what are its *affects*? From where does guilt originate?

Nietzsche understands guilt as a form of indebtedness and traces its origin to archaic forms of exchange, as between a debtor and creditor (1994). As human beings evolve culturally, this concrete feeling of indebtedness is sublimated into other higher beings such as family, spirits, state, gods, and God – God becomes the most abstract and highest symbol of guilt as He stands for the highest agency of 'crediting.' According to this understanding, 'I feel guilty' means I owe something, I am indebted to another and because of it I am insufficient, deficient, or in error, even if none of these may be true. All of this is determined by the 'crediting agency.' On the other hand, when a guilty party is sought, guilt can be externalizing. Let's keep in mind that guilt becomes more complicated as it becomes entrenched in its abstract forms, because it can become almost arbitrary. Along with the 'bad conscience' and every related, collectively repressed, human emotion, Nietzsche sees guilt as part of the civilizing process. Alternatively, Freud makes a distinction between external guilt and internal guilt (1961) and claims that internal guilt emerged in human history when the external authority figure was overthrown and an internal authority was implanted within the human psyche. This also corresponds to the rise of the superego, the agency that regulates human action. Guilt is then located in the superego of the soul and functions as the arbiter of allotment, that is, the regulator of what is 'owed' to whom or what, as the agency that accepts or rejects, and affirms or denies.

As guilt becomes more abstract and internalized, it is sublimated into higher, transcendental realms (God as the highest symbol of guilt, the most powerful creditor) and singular human lives become entirely arbitrary and fully at odds with their authentic needs. Rewards and punishments then become tools for a system of control that neither improves the individual nor society, which is the initial goal of this moral system. Now, under this internalized guilt, everyone feels guilty, everyone seeks the guilty, which is an underlying element of the panopticon as analyzed by Foucault.

In sport, a common trend one comes across is blaming others for defeat or mistakes when either really no person is to blame or when blame is collective. Insofar as ascertaining a guilty party is a function of our own internal guilt, this problem will not abate. To address this problem, guilt, its modulator crime/sin, and its end result in punishment, and their origin in human culture, must be examined, and their problems and complications in human life and interactions must be overcome. Two questions may guide us on the way: What do we 'owe' to higher powers such as ancestors and gods (the Nietzschean question), what is the significance of internalizing external authority, and what kind of authority is it (the Freudian question)? On the other hand, many scholars and historians have contrasted shame culture to guilt culture and revealed something in that opposition: in shame culture, the heroes who are autonomous but friends of the gods keep their word and excel in their actions as they are judged by their peers. When things go wrong, when a calamity befalls them, they come to see it as part of a fate determined by the gods, and often, they suffer alone, even if such suffering may take them to their ultimate end (as in the cases of Oedipus and Philoctetes). The tragic hero, or any ancient hero, may even commit suicide (a gesture of autonomy) rather than be dragged into misery or standards he considers inferior. In guilt culture, on the other hand, as one governed by God, the guilty party has no or very little autonomy (guilt is a sign of powerlessness), already feels burdened by guilt (often through ancestral guilt, guilt that he/she has not participated in making), and, therefore, is prone to find himself/herself and others guilty.

One such antidote to guilt may be shame, but we do not live in a shame culture any longer. We can perhaps learn from it, but, most importantly, we need to understand the origin of guilt and overcome those aspects of guilt that are antithetical to the spirit of sporting (as in blaming others when there is no one to blame). In most cases, especially in team sports, the blame of mistakes and losses falls on the entire team, including the coach. Instead of dwelling on loss, we need to learn from our mistakes and do our best to overcome them. Let's also not forget the role chance plays in life in general, and in sport. When it comes to luck and chance, there is no one to blame. In ball games, the bouncing ball does not 'a priori' favor any specific player.

Pity (compassion, empathy, sympathy, and the related)

Nietzsche, in contest with many previous philosophers, questioned the value of pity, whose status among human feelings he felt inferior, a critique that provoked much debate. The reason why Nietzsche problematized this basic human emotion is because it devalues the human being, it is a poor or lowly way of relation to the sufferings of others. I do not think that Nietzsche is opposed to relating to the sufferings of others, but only to those that appeal to the common denominator, or to our lower selves. The fundamental question Nietzsche raises in his works about pity is relevant to sport, or any other human interaction. In what ways can we relate to the suffering of others? Does such a relation elevate or demean human beings? That Nietzsche did not entirely disqualify pity should be clear from the different uses of the word *Mitleid* or *mitleiden*. What are the more elevating forms of *mitleiden* in the sporting context?

Some of the major sources of suffering in competitive sports are poor performance, defeat, and the plight of the athlete, which could be relatively innocuous, such as with an injury, or perilous, such as with cases of death. We can only sympathize with athletes who go through such suffering. However, for a star team to feel sorry for or pity the seemingly weak team, the underdog, may be dangerous, because they may have become stronger and may defeat the star team in the next play or game. Moreover, pity demeans those who are pitied and it is not an uplifting way of relating to others' suffering; it only aims to leave them at their impoverished or weak state. It is an insidious form of exercising power over others. Pitying the defeated team or athlete somehow implies that the victor will always remain a victor, which is far from the case. The victor too is susceptible to defeat in another round.

Pity that underestimates the power of the other could occur when there is a big disparity between opponents and almost everyone accepts the superiority of the strong no matter what. This is a speculation on my part, but Aleksander Karelin, all time wrestling champion from Russia, may have pitied his opponent, Rulon Gardner from USA, at the Sydney Olympics of 2000. Even Gardner did not believe that he could defeat Karelin, but he did (The Baltimore Sun, September 28, 2000).

Revenge (resentment and the like)

Revenge is payback, or preparation for payback, for a previous injustice. Payback, which Nussbaum lists as a condition of anger (2016: 28–29), is a psychic function and is often better than accepting loss and falling into despair and grief in the face of helplessness. If people believe in payback, whether it recovers anything good or not, they feel satisfied with it. But the act of payback does not accomplish much in the long run and for the greater whole; it boils down to self-satisfaction and is rooted in reactive feelings. What good does it do to punish a wrongdoer other than to satisfy one's own ego? Having my sibling's murderer executed will not bring my sibling back. One can argue that it is best to lock away the murderer so that the society at large will not be harmed any more. Yes, there is a point here, but why kill the murderer? There is no point there, but most people who lose a loved one tend to want to have the murderer executed. Furthermore, we are speaking of two different events and they need their own phenomenological understanding; the first act of injustice and the second act of revenge. Then we have the problem of mediated revenge, which takes up much psychic space and harms the revengeful[3] individual in the long run.

How does revenge play out in the sporting practice? First, at the more abstract level, athletes who are defeated may feel revengeful and may want to get back at those who defeated them in the next round.[4] This, however, does not fit into the way revenge is typically defined, because revenge almost always connotes a wrong-doing to begin with. There is no wrong-doing in defeating an opponent, as long as it is done fairly and according to the rules of the game. If the defeat was inflicted unfairly, if there is any cheating, game-fixing, or one-sided use of PEDs by some athletes, this may cause the feeling of revenge, not to mention anger and all the related feelings. It must be noted here that there could be gray areas for interpretation; in other words, the game may have been played fairly but the defeated interpret it as unfair game. This too can cause anger and revenge. Fouls and injuries, especially undue violence, can invoke revengeful feelings. There is no room for undue violence in non-combat sports. On the other hand, what are we to do with bullies who commit undue aggression, especially when their acts go unnoticed and undeterred by referees? Here the best option is to stand firm and strong and show the bully that his actions will not be tolerated. Any acts of mediated revenge, an undue foul against the bully, can create more problems than we would want to see: first, such acts may trigger the bully further, as he bullies more athletes; here we need to consider the unity of our team. Second, eye for an eye does not work in real life and does not work in sport. You will not bully your opponents simply because you were bullied. As Dixon observes, "violent retaliation is . . . an immature and intemperate response" (2010). Again, it is best that those whose function is to sustain a fair game, i.e. referees, do their job and do not allow any bullying and undue violent act so that such emotions of payback and revenge are not evoked.

Within the context of resentment, Fry brings up Nietzsche and his notion of 'ressentiment.' Let's keep in mind that Nietzsche's coinage of the term – Nietzsche retains the French form – refers to epochal settings and moral valuations and the notion has macro-level connotations. Slave morality, as stamped by 'ressentiment,' is a value-system that we have inherited from our past, which stands for life-negation, belief in one absolute truth, rejection of difference and diversity, body-denying and so on. Yes, it can be applied to power relations and micro-levels of culture, insofar as they pertain to relations between the weak and the strong and the haves and have-nots. And even, in this case, we have to exercise caution and not lose sight of Nietzsche's philosophy of the care of the self (in other words, the weak and the strong can point to trends that are within one's self). Therefore, as a third point here, Nietzsche's 'ressentiment' and resentment as used in English are not the same, even if they overlap. Having established these three points, let's ask the question Fry asks: can we cheer for the underdog without resentment and 'ressentiment'? Perhaps there are two questions here, but we will handle them together.

First, Fry convolutes *Schadenfreude* with resentment: "One further explanation is that people cheer for underdogs and upsets from a sense of *Schadenfreude*. We take joy in seeing the mighty fall"

(2017: 23). *Schadenfreude* is the joy one takes from the suffering of others; in Nietzsche, it is usually the strong that have this feeling in relation to the weak (gods as opposed to mortals); 'ressentiment' is an emotion that often resides in the souls of the weak in relation to the strong. But wouldn't it apply to the way Fry puts it? Would not people take joy in the defeat of a strong team and their subsequent suffering? Perhaps. Let's move on to the resentment part. "A Nietzschean take on this interpretation finds the key to this response in resentment . . . the slaves make a virtue of their weakness and vilify the strong. In this way, the slaves react in a convoluted, vengeful way." So far, so good, but the problem starts here: "No doubt Nietzsche's psychological genealogy uncovers a plausible role for resentment in cheering for the underdog" (2017: 23). First, Nietzsche's 'psychological genealogy' applies historically to the cultural field at large, specifically to the history of Occidental civilization and its highest values. Second, the sporting field, the field of competitive sport, is already an 'active' field, not a 'reactive' one. In other words, we are speaking of contest among more or less equal contestants; we are speaking of the actively strong and we need to look at them from the language of 'activity.' Why do you assume that the strong will suffer, the way the weak suffer, when they are defeated so that you can have your *Schadenfreude?* Finally, from the standpoint of Nietzsche's agonistic teachings as I present in my book, *Agon in Nietzsche* (2013), we have to fight against the stronger to be able to become strong, to be able to shed our weaknesses. From this standpoint alone, in a fair game of contest, one could support, in a Nietzschean spirit, the underdog without any resentment or 'ressentiment.' Therefore, I agree with Fry's conclusion but entirely for different reasons: "But there does not seem to be any logical necessity that cheering for the underdog should be motivated either exclusively or predominantly from resentment [or 'ressentiment']" (2017: 24).

Sadness

Sadness is an emotion that emerges in the face of loss. In sport, it may be due to losing a game, incurring an injury, or losing a teammate or an athlete especially when he or she is playing a game. There are many general coping mechanisms for loss; without these coping mechanisms sadness may turn into grief, its chronic, more intense form, and eventually depression. Sadness is a low-energy feeling. Once it takes hold of one's soul and body, it is hard to act unless one can shrug it off. One common form of depression in sport stems from injuries that prevent athletes from performing their sport activities. One example that I found is Kelly Holmes, the double Olympic champion in horse race at the 2004 Olympics of Athens. Prior to the games in Athens, Holmes suffered from leg injuries and fell into depression and started slashing her body with a pair of scissors. It seems like Kelly dealt with her sadness and depression after going through treatment before going to Athens (The Telegraph, May 30, 2005).

Shame

Shame is the most elusive of all emotions and perhaps the least understood. It goes right to the core of one's own being and has much to do with self-worth, dignity, how one is seen by others, and cultural practices of honor and prestige. Gilbert warns that shame should not be confused with preexisting conditions or post-shame effects and even with seemingly similar emotional states such as shyness, embarrassment, and guilt (1998: 4); shame is an unwanted and a difficult-to-control emotion, in a similar order like fear. Shame culture is often contrasted to guilt culture. In the former, public esteem is the greatest good and the code of honor is upheld throughout, within, and without. There is no separation between appearance and reality and between public and private. "They [members] form an honor-group: they expect certain types of behavior of themselves and others, and judge themselves and others accordingly." (Taylor 1985: 55). Loss of honor means loss of identity and end of that individual. Gods, as in *The Iliad*, are not part of this honor-society, but sit on top of them; they are the exemplary models of shame culture. In their case, shame does not bring their end (as in the case of Aphrodite caught with Ares in the act by her husband Hephaestus).

In ancient societies, especially the heroic ones, shame was an emotion that determined one's station in the hierarchical order. Heroes would act according to a heroic code of conduct so as to preserve their self-worth in the eyes of their peers, reinforced by their gods. The party that is shamed would have to restore his self-worth in one way or another; otherwise, he would lose his station. In sport, athletes are not necessarily shamed when they lose; humiliation may be the emotion that is often felt at loss, as McNamee observes:

Notwithstanding this, blowout scenarios, however various they may be, are not tied to shame necessarily. For, as we have noted above, shame is linked with a failure in reaching a designated moral as opposed to technical standard. In addition, there is nothing in losing by a large margin that would indicate the appropriateness of such a weighty emotion. One might say that embarrassment was the proper response to a failure against inferior opposition because of poor preparation. Shame will characteristically be thought too serious an emotional response. Yet if shame occupies itself with the transgression of issues of cultural, moral or religious rules, humiliation in its attenuated form is only tied to the conventional or the decorous. Many authors have noted that it holds a perversely incongruous grip on the psyche of some. One might think of those for whom humility had descended to the pathological. Instead of weighing their talents and achievements in a proper way, their self-evaluations never reach beyond mere self-loathing.

(McNamee 2008: 131)

On the other hand, shame is felt individually. How would every member of the losing team feel shame, if they upheld their code of honor throughout the game and played with valor? The main issue, however, is more than this: there are historic, socio-cultural dimensions of human emotions and we do not live in the hierarchical universe of shame culture. There are two parallel phenomena that are happening in the emotion of shame: the lowering of one's esteem in the eyes of one's self and, at the same time, in the eyes of a real or an assumed audience (of the same value sharing community).

As McNamee observes, shame may be too strong an emotion to feel in the face of defeat where there may be other emotional responses such as embarrassment or humiliation. All of these emotions, in different degrees, have to do with honor, who we are, our self-esteem and esteem in the eyes of others and our core values. In the sporting context, athletes may feel embarrassed or humiliated if expectations placed on them are high and if they underperform. One may feel humiliated in a defeat, but may come back and defeat the former victor. This is why shame, which is deeper, relatively permanent, and goes to the core of one's being, may be too strong an emotional response for defeat.

In conclusion for this chapter, most of the emotions discussed here are low-energy emotions, which can disturb or retard the spirit of competitive sport, with the exception of two: positive envy, relating to other's sufferings in an uplifting way (whether it is empathy or compassion) and shame. They are included here, because they are the antidotes (or counterparts) of emotions listed in this chapter: negative (or spiteful) envy, pity, and guilt.

Notes

1 There is no evidence of widespread suicide in sport. On the other hand, it would be difficult to conclude whether those athletes who attempted to or committed suicide did so due to sport-related reasons.
2 I have discussed this issue at length in a paper (Tuncel 2015).
3 Nietzsche makes a distinction between 'immediate' revenge and 'mediated' revenge in *Human, All Too Human*. In the former, one is strong enough to fight back against a harm, which, in fact, does not turn into a feeling of revenge. In the second case, one cannot respond and harbors the thought of retaliating against the person who inflicted harm (common among groups subjected to harm and mistreatment such as children, persecuted groups, etc.). This is what is properly called 'revenge.' Nietzsche's distinction is crucial to show the origin and the affect of revenge.
4 French uses the term 'revanche' for return game, which has very little to do with revenge as a human emotion. What I like in this usage is the transfiguration from the politics of war-making (this was how the term was used initially) to the playing field of sport.

Bibliography

Aristotle. (1994). *On Rhetoric: A Theory of Civic Discourse*. (transl. by G. Kennedy). New York: Oxford University Press.

Dixon, N. (2010). 'A Critique of Violent Retaliation in Sport'. *Journal of the Philosophy of Sport* 37:1, 1–10.

Freud, S. (1961). *Civilization and Its Discontents*. (ed. by J. Strachey). New York: W. W. Norton.

Fry, J. P. (2017). 'Underdogs, Upsets, and Overachievers'. *Journal of the Philosophy of Sport* 44:1, 15–28.

Gilbert, P. and Andrews, B. (1998). *Shame: Interpersonal Behavior; Psychopathology, and Culture*. Oxford: Oxford University Press.

Goldie, P. (2003). *The Emotions: A Philosophical Exploration*. Oxford: Oxford University Press.

Herzog, D. (2000). 'Envy'. In R. C. Solomon (ed.), *Wicked Pleasures* (pp. 141–160). Oxford: Rowman and Littlefield.

Hesiod. (2009). *Works and Days*. (transl. by M. L. West). Oxford: Oxford University Press.

Hobbes, T. (1969). 'Human Nature'. In D. D. Raphael (ed.), *British Moralists 1650–1800* (2 vols). Oxford: Clarendon Press.

McNamee, M. (2008). *Sports, Virtues and Vices.* London: Routledge.

Nietzsche, F. (1976). *The Portable Nietzsche.* (transl. by W. Kaufmann). New York: Penguin Books.

——. (1986). *Human, All Too Human.* (transl. by R. Hollingdale). Cambridge: Cambridge University Press.

——. (1994). *On the Genealogy of Morals.* (transl. by W. Kaufmann). New York: Vintage Press in Basic Writings of Nietzsche edited by W. Kaufmann.

Nussbaum, M. C. (2016). *Anger and Forgiveness: Resentment, Generosity, Justice.* New York: Oxford University Press.

Sartre, J.-P. (2007). *Existentialism Is a Humanism.* (transl. by C. Macomber). New Haven, CT: Yale University Press.

Sofia, R. and Cruz, J. F. A. (2016). 'Exploring Individual Differences in the Experience of Anger in Sport Competition: The Importance of Cognitive, Emotional, and Motivational Variables'. *Journal of Applied Sport Psychology* 28:3, 350–366.

Taylor, G. (1985). *Pride, Shame, and Guilt: Emotions of Self-Assessment.* Oxford: Clarendon Press.

Tuncel, Y. (2013). *Agon in Nietzsche.* Milwaukee, WI: Marquette University Press.

——. (2015). 'Defeat, Loss, Death, and Sacrifice in Sport'. *Journal of the Philosophy of Sport* 42:3, 409–423.

Web links

http://articles.baltimoresun.com/2000-09-28/sports/0009280100_1_gardner-rulon-fall-of-communism

https://en.wikipedia.org/wiki/Ice_hockey_at_the_1980_Winter_Olympics

www.theguardian.com/football/from-the-archive-blog/2015/jan/25/eric-cantona-kung-fu-kick-20-1995-archive

www.telegraph.co.uk/sport/othersports/athletics/2360388/Holmes-is-classic-case-of-athletes-depression.html

Chapter 7

Other specific feelings in sporting context

Ambition, euphoria, hubris, pride et al.

This chapter will be a continuation of the discussion on emotions that often appear or are subjects of discussion in the sporting context. Here I will focus on high-energy or upbeat emotions and their excess. Emotions are often considered as impediments or obstructions to meaningful interactions, but this is too simplistic a way of looking at emotions. Emotions can be positive even in intense conditions, as in competitive sports.

Ambition

Ambition is the fuel of any creative act, any meaningful action, without which not much could be done. In sport, the ambition to excel, to play well, to defeat one's opponent, to beat records propels athletes to better achievements; without this, they cannot achieve the higher goals which they had set for themselves and which are expected of them by their trainers, coaches, and fans. One has to strive higher and ambition underlies that strife, as Nietzsche underlies as a quality of the ancient Greek agonistic athlete.

I disagree with philosophers who consider ambition to be entirely negative and who argue against all ambition in sport or in general. However, ambition must have its limits; I am opposed to over-ambition rather than ambition itself; under-ambition, connected to lack of motivation, is as much a problem as over-ambition. Where do we draw the line? This may be the fundamental question, but there are no recipes for it, because every type of sport is unique, every game is unique, and every athlete is unique. What follows below are areas where athletes could be seen to be over-ambitious:

Within the field. Pretending to be the judge of the game or the coach of the team. Here athletes overstep their boundaries. The former case happens often when the players dispute the decision of the umpires when they are clearly on the wrong side (I am not suggesting that umpires are always right). The latter happens when athletes do not follow the wise and strategic instructions of their coaches and do what they will. Coaches see the whole team and the whole game while athletes often don't or can't because of the heat of the game or other reasons.

Another example for over-ambition is the tendency to win at all costs, no matter what. To commit fouls intentionally as one makes sure that he or she is not caught; fortunately, today's advance technology can catch what the bare eye cannot. Soccer, because of the size of the field and the high number of players, is perhaps the most susceptible to this *laissez-faire* trend in sport.

One final example for over-ambition is doping. This is a big topic to discuss here. I am not unconditionally opposed to performance enhancement drugs or anything that enhances performance; however, anything done that violates the rules of fair game or places some athletes at an advantage over others *hors de concours* destroys the spirit of sporting. What Lance Armstrong did not only violate the rules of the game, but went against the very reason of competing in cycling. He fell out of grace because of his *hubris*.

Outside the field. Athletes' response to spectators can often be excessive; yes, athletes are often provoked, but they should not respond to such provocations. Examples from the history of sport are plenty: the Indiana Pacers and Detroit Pistons basketball game in November 2004 when there were fights between Indiana Pacers players and Pistons fans; Cantona's attack against a fan in the match between Manchester United and Crystal Palace in 1995, because of some expletives that the fan threw at him (examples are from Farred 2014).

Euphoria (pleasure, joy, and the related)

Euphoria is a state of extreme joy, which can increase with more participants. One sees players and fans in euphoric states after a goal or a victory. The bigger the scale the higher is the intensity of euphoric expressions. What gives such joy to people has to be understood from the standpoint of their evaluation. Human beings are valued beings; their being becomes enhanced when the things they value and cherish grow, find recognition, and their powers are enhanced. In victory this is what happens to the team that wins. Euphoria and the related feelings are high-energy feelings associated with life-enhancing forces.

These are the feelings attributed to achievement, realization, perfection, etc. It is the feeling that comes with finishing a work; one can imagine when it is a teamwork followed by millions of people; your joy gets connected to their joy in an ocean of ecstasy.

In competitive sports, the victor's euphoria stands in a stark contrast to the sadness of the defeated team. There are not many cultural fields in which participants of the same community can feel incongruent emotions; competitive sport is one of them. Bring in mind the scene from the end of World Cup 2014 when Brazil was defeated, on its own turf, by Germany in the semi-finals. Some of the Brazilian players were crying on the field, in contrast to the joy of victory that the German players felt. Tears of different kinds were shed on the same field.

Different kinds of joy in sport and the problem of ersatz-experience

The joy of playing. The joy of playing a sport is a unique kind of joy that stems from being active and playful, winning – which is a sign of powerfulness – and being able to outsmart one's opponent (often associated with *metis*), or a combination of all. Its uniqueness becomes more complicated when we realize that the joy of sport includes toil, pain, and suffering. The first three, activity, playfulness, and powerfulness, go right to our primordial registers and are directly connected to our animal selves.

The joy of watching and the problem of spectatorship[1] (and the problem of active field of sport vs. the passive field of audience). The joy of watching a game stands in clear opposition to the joy of playing; for one thing, the latter is a form of activity, the former that of passivity. Spectatorship is not necessarily bound by rituals of the game, the way players are – not to mention the fact that we do not live in a ritualistic age. This disjuncture, which lies at the crux of our spectacular relations, creates a tremendous tension in the souls of the many; it is in this gap that fandom or herd-like hooliganism emerges in modern sports experience. Spectators' joy becomes a vessel for all social maladies; it becomes removed from the joy of activity and playfulness.

Honor

We do not live in honor societies any more, but this does not mean that we have no relationship to this primary human emotion. There are traces of honor or codes of honor in sporting practices, as McNamee observes:

> Nowhere is this better exemplified in late modernity than in the zero-sum structure of sports. And it is almost deified in sports such as boxing, where the language of the 'champion' and 'contender' is most obvious, where the claims to be 'the greatest' are the strongest. Honour though is not merely to be thought of as representing oneself appropriately in a social structure. It is noteworthy that, like other dispositions, honour predisposes us to feel and act in regular and interrelated ways. Those who value honour necessarily value reputation and above all the appearance of that reputation. A 'loss of face' is the modern vernacular for loss of honour. It follows then that how others see us is critical to our standing in the scheme of things.
>
> (McNamee 2008: 131)

Honor is about how one is esteemed by oneself and others at the same time; those others are one's peers against whom one is competing and with whom one shares the rituals and the code of honor. Now, honor is directly related to one's values, or the values shared by that community. In the sporting context, loss of face or loss of reputation can be tied to loss of honor; would defeat then be also connected to loss of honor? Typically, winning which brings reputation is associated with honor and losing with loss of honor, or shame.[2] Couldn't there also be honorable defeat? This subject becomes highly complex for at least two reasons: first, how do we assess the esteem an athlete deserves? The athlete can under- or overestimate his or her own worth and project it as such, although everything is out there for everyone to see in the field of competition, as McNamee observes (2008: 133). But no one sees those athletes who were not selected because they did not present their worth very well. Second, how are we going to assess the worth of athletes in team sports,[3] especially within the context of defeat? Perhaps many of the players, in that defeat, did their best, and played honorably according to their reputation, but their team still ended up with a defeat. Are they now supposed to lose honor? Can we lose honor collectively? If so, what does that mean? Does that mean that each one of us in the group has to lose honor so that we say the group lost honor? These are the complicated issues in our individual and collective experiences of emotion, as discussed in this book within the context of *affect* theory.

Hubris

One should not go beyond one's limits even in victory. This does not take away the joy of victory, but rather establishes a limit for it. There were measures set against *hubris* in ancient Greece. Gardiner translates hubris as insolence, sees 'aidos' as the feeling that counteracts hubris and defines it as follows: "the quality that wins him the favor of the gods and averts their jealousy . . . it is the feeling of respect for what is due to the gods, to one's fellow men, to oneself; the feeling of reverence, modesty, honor." (2002: 70). As I presented in *Agon in Nietzsche*, in Olympian VII, Pindar places prudence in opposition to hubris: "he goes in a straight course along a path that hates insolence; he has learned full well all the lessons prompted by the prudence" (2008: lines 90–95). In Hesiod's *Works and Days*, there are many warnings against hubris (2009: lines 210–240), which is discussed within the context of justice. In addition, there were many internal and external measures against hubris in the culture of agon: (1) gods did not like hubris; (2) hubristic acts were punished with ostracism as Nietzsche mentions in 'Homer's Contest' (1976: 39); 3) the 'epinician' odes could also have played a role of moderation for possible hubris on the part of the victor: instead of the victor praising himself, a poet did the eulogy; in this way the victor could afford or pretend to be modest (Tuncel 2013: 113–114). External measures, such as ostracism, would be used when internal measures such as shame, prudence, or moderation (*sophrosyne*) did not work. Even when others do the praising, one should exercise caution and not inflate the pomposity of the athlete (one cannot and should not overpraise a mortal). According to Nietzsche, hubris ends the ambition and envy, which fuel the cycle of competition, and may be the greatest danger waiting for the victor on the Olympic pedestal. (1976: 39).

For an athlete to go around and boast about being the best player outside the context of a specific game or a sport-related event is hubristic (there are many examples, but I will not list them here). For one thing, a human being cannot be the judge of himself or herself to be the best. The best judges of that specific sporting field have to determine who the best is. Second, such gestures are outward manifestations of megalomania for which ancient Greeks had antidotes. For us today, psychotherapy or psychoanalysis seems to be good options for the cure of such emotions (this is true for all of our emotional problems).

In today's world, there are many more factors than in the ancient world, which boast the egos of athletes, including material gain and mass media; these are the two major elements that compromise the spirit of sporting, as McNamee writes:

> What fuels hubris in sports, and what makes those who display the vice so ripe for humiliation, is the bloated importance of big-time commercialized sports and sportspersons. Too many veils of economic interest cloud the athlete's own critical self-interrogation. Irresponsible agents and journalists promote players in the most outrageous of styles. Florid language conduces to the formation of would-be heroic reputations based on the shifting sands of falsely conceived superhuman abilities. Athletes too often live a cocooned world where critical coaches and commentators can either be ignored or dismissed in favour of others who will sing more sycophantic songs.
>
> (McNamee 2008: 142)

McNamee then proposes humiliation as a corrective to hubris. I personally do not think this is sufficient, because humiliation takes care of the down side of the emotion but not its up-building side. In other words, athletes deserve to be joyful and prideful for their victories, but this pride should not take them to excessive pride or arrogance or allow them to show cases of pride *hors de concours*. Humiliation as a corrective addresses the latter but not the former. Moreover, the feeling of humiliation, whether it is weak or strong, can have regressive effects; this is antithetical to sport's perpetual motivation to excel. Ultimately, it boils down to power modulation and the best corrective is for athletes (and other members of the sporting community) *to know their place* in the hierarchy of the sporting world, even if it is shifting; in this way, they will neither under- nor overestimate their worth. As McNamee states: "In sports . . . greatness is indeed on loan temporarily from the gods" (2008: 144). With or without gods, I cannot agree more.

Hubris, depending on how it manifests itself, and what after psychoanalysis we may call nth order narcissism or narcissistic personality disorder, has negative impact on the sporting community. First, it complicates how one esteems one's self (complicates the feeling of pride). Second, it undermines the role of others, especially in team sports, in success. Third, it is an attempt to establish one's self as the best, as the victor for all times, where there is no such thing.

This attitude only undermines sport as a playful process. Coupled with over-ambition, hubristic trends can lead athletes to do all sorts of things to win no matter what. Perhaps the case of Lance Armstrong is an example for such hubris. Finally, it can create resentment among athletes, thereby complicating their relations.

Pride

Pride is one of those self-assessment emotions like humility, shame, and guilt and concerns the status of the self (Taylor 1985: 43). To have pride for oneself is the feeling of joy and increase of self-importance in the face of one's achievement and the object desired and is immediately connected to belief and value. On the other hand, not everything that gives us pleasure and joy leads to pride, a point which Hume struggles with. One other subject Hume (2000: Book 2, Part 1, Section VI) approaches regarding pride is the cause and the object of pride. The former ties in with the origin of the emotion of pride and the latter the object it takes. Here one can be proud of oneself or a specific possession or an achievement. To be proud of oneself with no reason or as a perpetual trait may close the doors for improvement and self-transformation. Hume also stipulated that the connection between the proud person and the object be close (and related). It does not make much sense if I am proud of the eagle that soars in the sky. But what about being proud of one's family members? Although there is proximity here, what exactly are we valuing in the family member, which and whom, respectively, we seem to be esteeming highly? Many hidden motivations may be implicated in such pride, not to mention the problem in esteeming someone highly *in toto*. Whether it is close or not, there is some sense of belonging to and valuation of something or someone in the emotion of pride. Therefore, pride operates between explanatory and identificatory beliefs, between causes and objects, objects esteemed by the person who is proud.

As long as pride is felt in its proper measure and celebrated in an appropriate manner, I do not see how it could be problematic. Those who warn against pride are cautious of potential and actual narcissism. But it is not the right path to fall into underestimation of one's worthwhile fighting against narcissism. The greatest challenge in the feeling of pride is to strike the right balance in appraising one's achievement. One must be truthful and not forget all the conditions that made one's victory possible; in team sports, the role of teammates is significant, not to mention the roles of trainers and coaches. On the other hand, in praising one's self one must be cautious not to fall into complacency and not to establish one's self as the victor before becoming so. In ancient Greece, others eulogized the victorious athlete, which took the burden of pride away from him; this was the function of 'epinicea,' which literally means 'around victory.' There were poets, like Simonides and Pindar, who wrote eulogies of victorious athletes and placed them in the context of their home history and myth. This already created a mythically bound eulogy, which, praising the athlete, restrained his pride to it. There is also the 'false' pride; we may be proud of things that we, in fact, did not achieve. In sports, games can be rigged or the referee may favor our team and help us win the game. Are we still going to be *proud* of our victory in such cases? Pride can go only so far; we can be proud of our own and real achievements, not more, not less.

On the other side of this subject, we can uphold that athletes are entitled to be proud of their achievements, just like others, as long as their pride is proportional to their achievement, no more, no less. No one, no team is the best for all eternity. The best is determined in the field for a specific game or round of games. No one can monopolize greatness. As McNamee notes, this is how Aristotle saw it:

> In Aristotle, we find an idea that jars on moderns: the idea that a certain level of pride is appropriate to those who are recognised for their greatness. Nevertheless, the idea that a certain status attaches to a role still remains in the strongly structured world of boxing as in other martial sports.
>
> (2008: 138)

Although the context in which he brings this up is boxing, it applies to all sports. I do not see why it should be jarring; the danger here is the thin line between pride and hubris.

Vanity

Is vanity an emotion or a specific way of being? Some would argue that vanity is not an emotion, because no one feels vain knowingly or expresses this feeling. I beg to differ; vanity, somewhat related to excessive pride, is an emotional propulsion to have one's self esteem in the eyes of others more than what one is. One difference between pride or hubris and vanity could be found in this: the excessively proud person has something to be proud of, but exceeds his/her limits whereas the vain person has little or nothing, but yet "seduces others to a false, much too high assessment of himself, yet then submits to the authority of these others" (Nietzsche 1986: 48). A politician, for instance, is utterly vain when he, through hand gestures, urges his audience to applaud him, as though what he were saying is gold whereas it could be rubbish. On the other hand, the vain may strive for positions of power to cover up their vanity.

Propensity to vanity increases in socio-cultural contexts where rewarding and admiring are of common occurrence, as in competitive sport. Human beings, however, become vain for different reasons. I listed one tendency; another one could be to compensate what is lacking in one's self. We watch superior athletes perform and become awe-struck simply because we can never do what they can. What they do looks like magic or miracle. This feeling little in and for oneself turns into a glorification of the athlete, analogous to the worshiping of heroes and gods in ancient times. The emptiness of the believer turns into a zealot defense of his icon, now he feels like his icon. He belongs to him; it is him. Vanity in this form is a compensation for what one does not have, what one can never have, and is endemic to modern fandom.

Final remarks for Part II

There was no logic, or no categories of distinction, in the creation of these chapters. The best way would have been to dedicate one chapter to each of the sport-specific emotions from A to Z, but giving a full treatment to each emotion in its own chapter would have made the book much longer and put its completion into an infinite horizon. Many of our emotions have their own place for our self-preservation; however, the culture of sport, especially competitive sport, which is my main focus, does not rest on the functions of self-preservation, but rather on the economies of self-transformation, transforming one's self toward higher states of being, which the concept of the Overhuman embodies. This higher self entails emotional transformation and achieving emotional 'maturity.' For each of the emotions I chose, I tried to show how some intense emotions can retard or betray the spirit of sport, such as rage, guilt, blame, hubris, revenge (retaliatory acts), grief, and despair, while some others uphold and uplift it. How athletes can cope with emotional problems and how emotions can be transformed is the subject matter of the next part.

Notes

1 I dealt extensively with the problems of spectacle in our age in my book, *Towards a Genealogy of Spectacle*. This is another area of hermeneutic circle where a field of culture reflects the problems of society and in return contributes to its formation.

2 One example for the loss of honor and the shame it induced from recent past is Kokichi Tsuburaya who "ultimately killed himself over his failure to win the Gold before his countrymen at the Tokyo Olympics" of 1968 (Lynne Belaief 1977: 55). Regarding this case (and other similar cases) we should exercise caution in coming to hasty conclusions, especially when we do not know the details.

3 There were no team sports in the Panhellenic games of ancient Greece. This still remains a puzzle to solve. One may look at this issue from a logistic perspective and suggest that the kinds of sports ancient Greek athletes played were not conducive to team sports; on the other hand, from an emotional standpoint, one could explain it by way of individualistic nature of the emotion of honor and shame.

Bibliography

Belaief, L. (1977). 'Meanings of the Body'. *The Journal of the Philosophy of Sport* 4:1, 50–67.

Farred, G. (2014). *In Motion, at Rest: The Event of the Athletic Body*. Minneapolis, MN: University of Minnesota Press.

Gardiner, N. E. (2002). *Athletics of the Ancient World*. Mineola, NY: Dover.

Hesiod. (2009). *Works and Days*. (transl. by M. L. West). Oxford: Oxford University Press.

Hume, D. (2000). *A Treatise of Human Nature*. (ed. by D. F. Norton and M. J. Norton). Oxford: Oxford University Press.

McNamee, M. (2008). *Sports, Virtues and Vices*. London: Routledge.

Nietzsche, F. (1976). *The Portable Nietzsche*. (transl. by W. Kaufmann). New York: Penguin Books.

——. (1986). *Human, All Too Human*. (transl. by R. Hollingdale). Cambridge: Cambridge University Press.

Pindar. (2008). *The Complete Odes*. (transl. by A. Verity). Oxford: Oxford University Press.

Taylor, G. (1985). *Pride, Shame, and Guilt: Emotions of Self-Assessment*. Oxford: Clarendon Press.

Tuncel, Y. (2013). *Agon in Nietzsche*. Milwaukee, WI: Marquette University Press.

Part III

Care of emotions

Our emotional make-up needs its own proper care, the way our bodies and minds need theirs. Moreover, every type of emotion needs its own care. But what does 'care' really mean? We are born with basic human emotions along with a bundle of instincts and drives. Pain and pleasure, joy, and suffering, regulate much of our early development, as we come to absorb the emotional make-up of our immediate surroundings. Yes, emotions pass on to new generations, because they are coded in the values, ideologies, and beliefs of what surround us. We grow up to feel rage, jealousy, envy, and other emotions, according to them. We inherit problems as we inherit these values, which codify emotions. We internalize the outside world, relationships that we see around ourselves and relationships that embody human emotions.

In this last part of the book, I want to understand how as members of the sporting community we can work on our emotional make-up. In the first chapter of this part, I focus on the intrinsic components of the sporting field and figure out what can effect emotional transformation in a positive direction especially among young athletes and with a focus on training. This chapter highlights, in a Humean spirit, the significance of being emotionally developed and mature. In the second chapter, I explore how disciplinary approaches, whether they are from philosophy, medicine, psychology or psychoanalysis, can be utilized to understand human emotions and address their problems in sporting practice. Here coping mechanisms come into play. Finally, in the third chapter I try to comprehend the intricate relationship between emotion and action.

Chapter 8

'Sentimental education'[1] of athletes

We cannot underestimate our emotional needs and the problems that stem from them. In order to have healthy relationships with ourselves and with others in the sporting community, it is necessary to deal with 'raw' or repressed emotions.

Many outbursts and excessive behaviors in sport, very common in ice hockey, for instance, could be done to create a spectacle, to entertain spectators, but these are only cheap effects and have very little to do with sporting culture. Sport fans, their boredom and need for amusement and entertainment should not impact the culture of sport; yes, there are antecedents for this in the Roman culture of gladiators, but such things were not accepted in ancient Greek sport, the origin of Olympic games. Sport spectatorship too needs to be held to higher standards and we need to reverse the dualistic pattern of active spectacle (the sporting field) vs. passive spectatorship (the empty bored fandom) by investing in a pervasive sport culture so that spectators are in tune with the sporting field, as though they too were athletes. This, no doubt, necessitates an active sport culture.

Emotional formation

Athletes have a unique opportunity to work on their emotions, because sport is one of those fields in human life which brings out emotions, especially intense emotions from anger and anxiety to pride and euphoria.

Transformation of 'raw' emotions

Human beings are like *pu*, uncut wood,[2] to be worked on. Our first emotional responses to our environment are often copies of that environment at unconscious levels. Just like other things that are human, we imitate, we get angry for no good reason or false reasons, we become envious of material goods that we have no real need for, we become jealous, and we may become mean-spirited. Or, under robust conditions, we may be lucky to be bestowed with uplifting emotions. Our world today is full of conditions for reactive, negative emotions, but this is no reason to be a pessimist; poor conditions of living, poor standards of education/formation, systems of prejudice, and abuses are rampant in our age, all of which are conditions for such negativity. In short, we replicate what is around us; we replicate all the reactive emotions that we inherit from our 'Lebenswelt.' What I would like to present below is a series of emotions that can be transformed and cultivated in sport from the ground up, despite all odds, despite all negativity coming either from society itself or from the sporting field.

Motivation for life and life goals. What is often called 'chutzpah' or what the medievals called 'effective grace,' not having it or having less would put people in a vegetative state and having too much could turn them into zealots. On the other hand, it is crucial to be motivated in life for which one needs to have goals and passions; psychologists work on this goal. One theory in psychology related to motivation is Self-Determination Theory (SDT), which is "based on the premise that individuals have innate tendencies toward psychological growth and development, to master ongoing challenges and, through their experiences, to develop a coherent sense of self" Jones and Kingston 2013: 51). Intrinsic motivation is central to this theory and describes an inclination toward "assimilation, mastery, spontaneous interest and exploration" (Jones and Kingston 2013: 51). Many studies in sport sciences show that coaches who support athletes' autonomy are more effective in supporting athletes' motivation than those who do not. To support athletes' autonomy means to acknowledge their feelings and perspectives, involve them in the decision making process, avoid controlling behaviors, minimize pressure and other unnecessary constraints, while providing positive feedback (Jones and Kingston 2013: 52).

Anxiety/fear in performance. This subject was dealt with previously, but within this context, I would add that it is necessary for every athlete to understand his/her deep-seated fears. The ultimate fear may come from our fear of death or from being treated unjustly and dishonorably. Fear can also stem from underperforming, being judged by others, superiors, and fans, being dismissed from a game or a team and ultimately from losing a game and being eliminated in the selection process. We cannot be alone in dealing with all these fears, but we can do what falls on our shoulders based on our roles in the sporting community. Sport psychologists have developed techniques to deal with somatic and cognitive anxieties such as progressive-muscular relaxation and techniques of thought stopping and positive thought control, respectively (Jones and Kingston 2013: 60).

As for high-level performance, an indication of motivation and overcoming of inhibitive anxiety, a recent psychological study from 2010 done on elite athletes highlighted mastery, demonstration of ability, physical/mental preparation, and social support as the most important sources used by athletes prior to their sporting events (Jones and Kingston 2013: 57).

Anger for what. Anger is a common human emotion, felt and expressed for a variety of reasons. It is an emotion of discontent or disagreement. Trainers, coaches, umpires/referees, and organizers need to do their best to remove conditions of anger from the field and the game, and interfere where necessary. For coaches to support their athlete when he or she is clearly in the wrong and unjust is the worst thing that can be done to the culture of sporting; unfortunately, this is a common trait that still persists. On the other hand, umpires have to be more attentive and uphold the fair game at all times. Recent technologies can benefit them in this way (ancient Greeks used many gadgets to ascertain fair play, although they did not have today's advanced technologies). Things like discomfort and stress often create conditions for anger and outbursts of anger. Psychologists propose: (a) primary-level interventions which concern the elimination of the stressors encountered by athletes in their performance environments (in training and competition); (b) secondary-level interventions which have to do with stress management training; and (c) tertiary-level interventions which "involve the treatment of problems once they have occurred" (Jones and Kingston 2013: 64).

Envy for whom and what. Envy expresses a lack of something and a desire to possess it. There are loftier beings, objects, rewards, and levels of achievement that are worth envying and the envy we have can propel us to these higher goals. However, envy out of context, spiteful envy, and envy for goals that cannot be achieved or can be achieved over a long period of time will not only frustrate us within but also complicate our relations to others. Unfortunately, the obsession with material wealth and gross inequities in distribution of wealth and income complicates the lives of many people and confounds or exacerbates their feeling of envy. Sport, insofar as it is a field of competition of talents, can keep its distance to spiteful envy. I must add here that material wealth has a long history of complicating the spirit of competitive sport, although in recent times it has become a chronic problem. In ancient Greece, there was a shift from stephanitic to chrematitic games (see Tuncel 2013: 243–247), which is emblematic of the interference of material gain into the symbolic and honorable gain of victory.

Go easy with blame. Blaming others is a common human trait. It deflects the problem from ourselves and projects it onto others. Based on this depiction, it is egoistic; however, the feeling of guilt is more complicated than the simple blaming of others. Nonetheless, such blaming does no good either to ourselves or to our team. It can only demoralize and anger those who are blamed out of context.

The role of trainers and coaches as arbiters of emotional experiences in their teams

Diagnosis of the problem. The first people who come in contact with athletes are trainers and coaches and they are also the first to witness emotional problems as they emerge in sporting context. Even before emotional problems may appear, often in the form of a conflict among athletes, many signs appear in the form of gestures, facial expressions, bodily postures, hand or foot gestures, etc. Darwin (1872/1998) gives many hints about these types of non-verbal expressions of emotion. It is possible that trainers and coaches too have emotional problems or perpetuate these problems in their teams. They will then be a problem in the equation rather than its solution. Furthermore, assuming that coaches are in touch with their own emotions, after Darwin and William James, there have been many studies on bodily and facial expressions of emotions from which they can benefit to read the cues of their athletes; one recent book is Beatrice De Gelder's *Emotion and the Body*, which places all somatic emotional signs in a context. She shows how we have been obsessed with facial expressions in the West, because the face is what we immediately see, whereas the main issue is the body. The entire human body is not only a repository of all emotions but it is also a great field of emotional signs, yes, including the face.

Elimination of the problems in the field (conditions that produce negative emotions). In many instances of human interaction, circumstances create a milieu conducive to negative emotions which can be eliminated with wise decisions.

Preparation of athletes for ordeals and difficulties; regimes of strength. Sport is a field of empowerment in which one sheds one's weaknesses and becomes stronger in his/her specific field. Becoming strong has received a bad name because of its implications in politics (and in thought in the form of social Darwinism) and also because of its by-products, both of which stem from a lack of understanding how power works and the different *Gestalts* that it takes.

Acceptance of one's self and strife for one's higher self. Sport is one area where the care of the self occurs not only in our physical being but also in other fields. Sport is a way of socializing; for team sports, it is a way of coopting with others. It gives the members of the sporting community a chance to work on and improve their selves. That improvement, however, passes through emotional maturation. Without such maturation, sport can also expand and multiply social ills.

Who is to judge?

To be able to judge the emotional maturity of others, one must be more mature than them at least in those emotions that are under consideration (here I have only sport-specific emotions in mind). Otherwise, we will have the dilemma of assessment, as Adam Smith highlights in a passage in his *The Theory of Moral Sentiments* (19). First, we judge according to the faculties we have (this was Smith's point); second, we can judge if we have something similar; and third, when we judge we stand at a higher footing than what is being judged (this is my point).

Umpires/referees as arbiters of emotional experience on the field and the question of active vs. reactive justice

Nietzsche develops his notion of 'activity' in opposition of 'reactivity' in *On the Genealogy of Morals*, First Essay. What is reactive is that which rejects difference and diversity according to an absolute truth, *the* absolute truth[3] in the mind of the reactive;[4] it is also, at the outset, hostile to life and all the life forces; the feeling that is associated with this state of being is 'ressentiment.' On the other hand, "the reverse is the case with the noble mode of valuation: it acts and grows spontaneously, it seeks its opposite only so as to affirm itself more gratefully and triumphantly" (1994: 473). Spontaneous means not just in theory, but rather in action; the noble athlete seeks his opposite in contest and is grateful for that and may be victorious in that seeking. In addition, what typifies the noble is an affirmation of life and passion (of the body, its growth and different states), a distinction of rank and file (between the victorious and the defeated), an almost inborn sense of well-being, trust (in oneself), openness (toward one's self and one's opponents) and uprightness, and desire to have one's own opponents. Nietzsche's general description of the noble notwithstanding, all of these qualifications can be observed in the contestant.

Furthermore, Nietzsche's extensive discussion of justice, and specifically active vs. reactive justice, unfolds in the Second Essay of *The Genealogy*. First he uncovers an archaic layer of human history in the transactions of exchange and in the matter of justice, which to him is "the good will among parties of approximately equal power to come to terms with one another, to reach an 'understanding' by means of a settlement" (1994: 506–507).[5] Here what is decisive is the contest of powers, the custom of comparing, measuring, and calculating power against power. As the human civilization advances and societies become stronger, a consciousness of power evolves that allows the transgressor, that is the debtor who cannot pay his debt back, go unpunished; this, for Nietzsche, is a transformation of justice into mercy, which remains to be the privilege of the most powerful. These preliminary remarks on the so-called primitive layers of human development prepare the stage for Nietzsche to attack Dühring or others who seeks the origin of justice in 'ressentiment,' reactive feelings, or any form of retribution.

Having shown the origin of justice in power relations among more or less equals, Nietzsche counteracts, with his own position, Dühring's position,[6] which seeks the origin of justice in the sphere of reactive feelings, as he asserts that the sphere of reactive feelings is the last sphere to be conquered by the spirit of justice. We may leave Nietzsche's optimistic tone aside, namely that humanity started with a sense of active justice but later was corrupted by reactive justice, and proceed to examine what he means by active justice:

> The just man remains just even toward those who have harmed
> him . . . when the exalted, clear objectivity, as penetrating as
> it is mild, of the eye of justice and *judging* is not dimmed even
> under the assault of personal injury, derision, and calumny, this
> is a piece of perfection and supreme mastery on earth.
>
> (1994: 510)

The description may very well fit an athlete who remains just and
upholds the fair rules of the game despite all personal injuries and
ordeals. Furthermore,

> the active, aggressive, arrogant man is still a hundred steps closer
> to justice than the reactive man; for he has absolutely no need to
> take a false and prejudiced view of the object before him in the
> way the reactive man does and is bound to do.
>
> (1994: 511)[7]

In the next sentence Nietzsche adds other qualifications[8] to the active
type: strength, nobility, courage, freer eye, and better conscience. The
active type is closer than the reactive type to justice as Nietzsche
understands justice in its origin, that is, 'active justice.' We must,
however, dig deeper into the conditions of active justice: the active
type accepts the diversity of life, the diversity of opponents as in
contest, is aggressive toward them in proper doses and in its own
proper place, crosses over unto opponents, is trained to be strong
and exhibits qualities of strength, is courageous in struggle, has a
freer eye to judge fairly, and does not internalize (i.e. repress) animal instincts. Although it is implicit in what is already said, it is
necessary to underline that active justice is a type of justice that
takes the body and the human animal into account.

Finally, justice for Nietzsche is not just a concept, is not an empty
word that is regurgitated endlessly. It is not a virtue that, removed
from its vital source, puts people to sleep, nor is it an ideal that
lives in a neverland but rather *lives* here on earth. It is rather a
lived reality of a people as it is manifest in its practices and institutions and as it is determined in strength and promotes strength; it
is the type of justice as practiced in the *agonal* acts both among
the approximately equal contestants and in the power of judgment
of the umpires of contest. The paradigm for justice for Nietzsche
must be this type of active justice, justice as a mediation among
the strong, and all other forms of justice (mediation for retribution

and for mundane affairs), albeit Nietzsche's easy dismissal of them, must be placed under the hierarchy of active justice. As in all things, the strength and the superiority of the best that contest upholds and promotes and the ennoblement of great moments and struggles must reign. The teachings of Zarathustra confirm this idea and practice of active justice when he exhorts judges not to turn a sublime moment into baseness: "That he judged himself, that was his highest moment; do not let the sublime return to his baseness!"[9] This model of active justice based on strength, as typified by the agonist whether a contestant or a judge of contest and as removed from revenge, speaks across generations.

How to uphold justice in sport

Fairness and justice. Many of us in the sporting field agree that fairness must be upheld at all times in sport; favoritism, wrong judgment, bribed judges, and rigged games will destroy the spirit of sport, if not for all sport, but at least for that particular game. We may also accept the fact that only certain types of persons can be judges in sport and we can hope for that, as McFee writes "At least we can recognize the need for judges . . . to be knowledgeable, informed, sensitive to the game" (2004: 240). I must also add that the judges must be able to uphold 'active justice' as I described above. This in itself goes against the kind of justice we are accustomed to on the grander scale, because the political justice we practice is 'passive justice' based on revenge and retribution. This is why analogies between the rules of sport and political laws do not make any sense. There is a disparity between the types of justices that are at work. There is a stark difference between a judge who gives a life-effecting punishment to a criminal for a single offense, presumably for the order of society (this in itself can be debated) and an umpire who punishes an athlete for not upholding the rules of that game only for that game. In the former case, it is the society's revenge on a single individual, whereas the latter is for the sake of the spirit of sporting when it is fairly implemented.

Upholding the rules of the game. I agree with Vampley that "sport needs rules" and "rules matter" (2007: 843–844) and rules are created by human beings and they change. He mentions the diffusion of a sport for why rules matter, but more importantly there would not be any fair game if there were no rules, not to mention a framework for players to play, whether these rules are explicit or implicit. Vampley then goes on discussing three different types of rules in sport, namely, constitutive, auxiliary, and regulatory (2007: 845). Where I disagree with Vampley is not regarding what he says about rules in sport, but rather the way he sidesteps fairness in sport: "Today, especially at the elite level, fair play might be seen as an anachronism" (859). For one thing, fair game goes as far back as ancient Greeks if not further back, not just to the Victorian age (857). On the other hand, if it were not for fair play, there would not be any sport. The desire to win in a contest game does not necessarily violate the rules of fair game, but rather the desire to win at any cost.

The role of technology. As Harry Collins observes, TV has complicated the relationship between the ontological authority and the epistemological privilege of the umpire: "Television reveals that umpires occasionally make wrong decisions" (2010: 139). The same technology can be used by a committee of umpires, some of whom watch the game in real time and negotiate the sporting judgment with the on-field umpire, as in rugby. Other technologies are RTDs (2010: 140). I agree with Collins that the question of exactness should not be confounded with the question of justice (2010: 144); nor is the implementation of justice to be confused with its spirit. The former has to do with logistics, with the position of the umpire, etc. and the visibility of the game in action while the latter goes right to the core of the spirit of sporting. We live in a technological world where the effects of technology are not always positive and not contributing to healthy practices. Sport is one of those fields of culture where, though not a field of technology itself, is infused with technology and has an impact on the emotional aspect of sports. What I propose in the preceding text is to put technology in the use of active justice. There are, however, many areas in sport where the use of technology often erodes the spirit of sporting, as in mass media representation of sports and one-sided, out of context, use of performance enhancement drugs.

To conclude, emotions can elevate us and take us to higher goals or they can take us down the drain. Human beings are unique bundles of emotions, most of which are like uncut or unworked wood (*pu* in Taoism). We get angry at the smallest, worthless things; we envy material things for which we have no real need; we become revengeful although no revenge can undo the initial harmful act; we start boosting our ego at the first opportunity of victory; we fall into despair at the slightest defeat . . . and so forth and so on. There are many ways to work on the uncut wood without creating vicious circles in the traps of affectivity.

Notes

1 This phrase, though borrowed from Flaubert, was suggested by Cesar Torres at the 43rd annual IAPS conference in Cardiff (2015). It fits very well with this theme and I thank him for the suggestion.

2 The term is borrowed from ancient Taoism in which every human being is considered potentiality to be worked on.

3 For the reactive (of the slave morality or the morality of good and evil) there is only one absolute truth and all else is to be judged and condemned based on this one Truth; whereas for the active (of the master morality or the morality of good and bad), there are many truths and hierarchy of goods and bads in a given constellation (Nietzsche's seeming dualism is only heuristic and does not suggest an ontological dualism in morality). According to the latter, there are many diverse paths and diverse truths. This polysemic aspect of what is true stems from the nature of polytheism and is often expressed by the poets: "Various men excel, indeed, in various ways; but it is meet that man should walk in straight paths, and strive according to his powers of nature" (Pindar N-I, 25–30). And Bacchylides: "Each man seeks a different road to glory . . . We all tread different paths" (Ode X). We are different and tread different paths, but agree and come together to strive higher in the fields that conform to our *physis* and honor that struggle. This is the teaching of the 'agonal' poets and their age.

4 There is also a reactive type of justice that Nietzsche critiques; the underlying feeling of this type of justice is revenge (revenge of a certain kind, that of impotence) because its aim is to equalize that which is unequal (the weak and the strong alike). This is the justice of the rabble (its revenge against the strong) as the tarantula symbolizes this type of revenge:

> The tarantulas, of course, would have it otherwise. 'What justice means to us is precisely that the world be filled with the storms of our revenge' – thus they speak to each other. 'We shall wreak vengeance and abuse on all whose equals we are not' – thus do the tarantula-hearts vow.
>
> (*Zarathustra* II: "On the Tarantulas" 2005: 211–212)

Zarathustra calls this the 'tyrannomania of impotence.' In contrast, active justice aims to hold together the striving, strong types in their agonistic relation and organizes the strong and the weak in a hierarchical relationship.

5 An older version of this idea of justice among approximately equals was presented in *Human, All Too Human* Aphorism 92. There Nietzsche had not yet arrived at a notion of 'active justice,' but the agonistic overtones are clearly present:

> *Origin of justice.* – Justice (fairness) originates between parties of approximate *equal power*, as Thucydides grasped (in the terrible

colloquy between the Athenian and Melian ambassadors): where there is no clearly recognizable superiority of force and a contest would result in mutual injury producing no decisive outcome the idea arises of coming to an understanding and negotiating over one another's demands: the characteristic of *exchange* is the original characteristic of justice.

Here Nietzsche is thinking the question of justice in a general way with agon symbolism, while in the practice of 'agon' there is a decisive outcome.

6 In the beginning of this section, Nietzsche camps the psychologists of 'ressentiment,' like Dühring, with the anarchists (who believe that all are equal, that all power is corrupt, and dismiss all hierarchy) and the anti-Semites who reject Jews at the outset because of their difference and are therefore reactive.

7 In the original: "Der active, der angreifende, der übergreifende Mensch" which translates as "the active, the attacking, the overlapping or crossing-over human being." We must imagine two boxers, wrestlers or pankratists or American football player who constantly cross over into one another during the game. Kaufmann's translation 'arrogance' for *übergreifende* does not make any sense in this context.

8 In some of these qualifications Bertram sees a biological determination and sophistic elements in Nietzsche. Discussing the same passages he writes:

> Here Nietzsche clearly approaches the biologically determined, dialectically refined conception of justice that the Greek sophist Thrasymachus advances in Plato's Republic when he defines what is just as that which benefits the stronger and what is unjust as something more powerful, noble, and mighty than justice.
> (Nietzsche: Attempt at a Mythology, 81)

It is not clear to me how Nietzsche's active justice that takes a noble and a bodily affirmation of life in contest as its starting point resembles Thrasymachus' benefit oriented sense of justice (the benefit idea is repeated throughout his arguments). On the other hand, the biological determination must not be accepted *prima facie*. It is not only the body and the life forces that are determining in themselves for Nietzsche, but rather what human beings do with them in their own cultural constellations. The Greeks of the *agonal* age *created* cults, institutions, and practices (acts of culture) to allow for bodily *freedom* and discharge of animal instincts (acts of the body). In this way they revered the sacred animal in man.

9 'On the Pale Criminal' in (2005).

Bibliography

Collins, H. (2010). 'The Philosophy of Umpiring and the Introduction of Decision-Aid Technology'. *Journal of the Philosophy of Sport* 37:2, 135–146.

Darwin, C. (1872/1998). *The Expression of the Emotions in Man and Animals*. (ed. by P. Ekman). New York: Oxford University Press.

De Gelder, B. (2016). *Emotions and the Body*. New York: Oxford University Press.

Flaubert, G. (2004). *Sentimental Education*. (transl. by R. Baldick). London: Penguin Classics.

Jones, R. L. and Kingston, K. (2013). *An Introduction to Sports Coaching: Connecting Theory to Practice*. New York: Routledge.

McFee, G. (2004). *Sport, Rules and Values: Philosophical Investigations into the Nature of Sport*. London: Routledge.

Nietzsche, F. (1994). *On the Genealogy of Morals*. (transl. by W. Kaufmann). New York: Vintage Press in Basic Writings of Nietzsche edited by W. Kaufmann.

———. (2005). *Thus Spoke Zarathustra*. (transl. by G. Parkes). Oxford: Oxford University Press.

Plato. (1992). *The Republic*. (ed. by C. D. C. Reeve and transl. by G. M. A. Grube). Indianapolis, IN: Hackett Publishing Co.

Smith, A. (1790/1976). *The Theory of Moral Sentiments*. (ed. by D. D. Raphael and A. L. Macfie). Oxford: Clarendon Press.

Tuncel, Y. (2013). *Agon in Nietzsche*. Milwaukee, WI: Marquette University Press.

Vamplew, W. (2007). 'Playing with the Rules: Influences on the Development of Regulation in Sport'. *The International Journal of the History of Sport* 24:7, 843–871.

Chapter 9

Therapeutic treatment of emotions in sporting practice

Therapy means healing (the root is the Greek verb *therapeuin*); for healing to start the problem has to be diagnosed first. Unlike physical symptoms, emotional symptoms are often invisible, they don't always give signs until they are burst open. Someone who has anger issues may not show signs until the moment strikes for him to burst into rage; in contrast, most physical problems do give signs, especially in the form of pain. To complicate things further, many refuse to accept their emotional problems because they see such recognition as weakness. They don't realize that what makes them weak is their emotional immaturity rather than its recognition. What interests me most in this topic is how athletes and other members of the sporting community can deal with and heal their emotional problems. I do not dismiss the role of uplifting emotions in sport; for example, the need for an athlete to be in the right mood and the right emotional state, before competition. However, here I will focus on the healing process of so-called negative emotions, emotions that could disrupt or destroy the spirit of sporting.

For athletes to deal with their emotional problems their sporting community must act in unison, because we hang together in our problems. The following are some approaches to address emotional problems.

Integral approach

How are all emotions related? Can we work on a single emotion? One approach (most classical schools of thought) maintains that emotions belong together and we cannot fix the problems of a single emotion, because at bottom they stem from the same source, the human character, and the human soul is unitary. A rageful, a revengeful or a 'hubristic' person is already poor in character; such persons need to work on all of their emotions to be better persons.

This approach, however, is limited; first, it does not consider the uniqueness of each human emotion. There is no causal relationship among emotions. An angry person is not necessarily a revengeful person. Anger and revenge are not the same, even if they may be conjoined at times. Second, it does not consider the intensity of emotions; anger may not be a problem if expressed in its proper dose, but a problem if it exceeds its appropriate limits. Third, it does not accept the multiplistic root of emotions at the psychosomatic level of *affects*. Finally, it does not recognize other distinctions that could apply to emotions, such as low-level and high-level emotions.

How to approach emotions individually and integrally?

Do we treat emotions singly or do we consider the entire emotional make-up of a human being? Single emotions: anger issues, or being over-ambitious or being guilt-ridden. Each type of emotion needs its own care. On the other hand, some people may be introverted and emotionally unexpressive. This is not to say that in every case of such withdrawal they are dealing with their emotions internally. More often than not they are becoming kegs of gunpowder ready to explode. The fundamental question from the standpoint of caring for emotions is whether a particular emotion can be isolated from the rest and dealt with in that isolation; or, when healing emotions, one has to consider the total human being with all his/her emotions.

How to deal with stress and trauma?

Much of the psychological literature on this topic of stress in sport presents coping mechanisms for emotional issues. The last 25 years or so have yielded many studies. One model developed by Anshel (1990) is COPE, an acronym for the four steps proposed: Control emotions, Organize input, Plan response, and Execute the next action (Delaney 2016: 'Cognitive Control Strategies and Sportsman-ship' 102–104). Stoppage, countering, and reframing are the three major cognitive strategies listed; the first one is the use of a trigger word, the second one has to do with internal dialogue and the last one involves taking in and processing information in a positive way. They are all functions of the mind.

Coping with emotions

Coping with emotions has many different dimensions. The first one has to do whether one is ready to deal with an emotion or not. Here the distinction is the actual coping with an emotion and the potential to deal with it; the latter has to do with "an evaluation of prospects for coping" (Thatcher, Jones, and Lavallee 2014: 39). Such coping potentials, 'emotional maturity' in my own terminology, often influence emotional experiences of athletes in a positive way. The other dimension has to do with the direction or the object of coping: "Problem-focused coping involves taking action to change an aspect of the person – environment relationship, either by altering an aspect of the environment itself, or by changing one's situation within it." (Thatcher, Jones, and Lavallee 2014: 39). On the other hand, 'emotion-focused coping' involves redirection of attention or a reinterpretation of the athlete's relationship with his/her environment.

One difficulty in coping with emotions is to first diagnose the problem. Here the problem may originate from the self or from others; the former demands work on one's self, the latter on collective healing. Second, every emotion needs its cathartic discharge; a sad event like a loss of a game or a teammate demands its time for mourning, for instance. Third, there are times when we are lost in our emotions, as in anticipation and expectation in a major international game. We are neither in a pleasurable nor in a painful state; rather, in a mixed state. On the other hand, uncertainty may intensify an emotion, as Hume observes (2000: 441–442). Finally, mixed emotions, not as just mentioned but in general, may be too difficult to assess and address. Mixed emotions become intense when opposite intense feelings such as joy and suffering come together in such a way that they pull that person apart.

Psychoanalytic approach

Much of the cognitive approach focuses on what the mind can do consciously and actively, but does not consider some of the psychic phenomena that lie at the depths of the human soul, more specifically, at unconscious levels. It is easier to work at the levels of consciousness, but far more difficult at unconscious levels. For instance, I can remove myself from training if I get angry at my teammate, but this does not mean that I have dealt with my anger issues that are rooted in my psychosomatic being. Psychoanalysis too has many branches, but all psychoanalytic movement acknowledges the unconscious and, depending on its method, creates the analytic milieu in which the analyzed deals with psychic problems at their deeper levels, including their imagistic and symbolic constellations. More will be discussed on this approach below.

Approaches based on discipline

Philosophical approach

Through reflection, meditation, and discussion, philosophers have brought much about human emotion to surface. Most schools of philosophy have their own theory of emotion. In Part I of this book, I have discussed some of these theories; however, if we include all traditions, in all literature, Western and non-western, we will discover an endless wealth of ideas. Two trends have appeared in Western thought, which are highly problematic; one of them is dismissive of emotions. Dismissal can take on a variety of forms. The other one promotes the idea of mental control of emotions as one finds in Stoicism. The mental control cannot always be possible, is not always desirable (there are times when emotions must be expressed), and negates the entire project of focusing on particular emotions and their qualitative refinement, or what may be called 'sentimental education.'

However, thinking about an emotion in the abstract would not contribute much to the healing of that emotion at the individual level. What needs to be considered here is a form of thinking that is in touch with emotions and in touch with psychosomatic functions; let's call this type of thinking 'intuitive thinking.' Therefore, I am proposing a form of thinking that enables us to be in touch with ourselves and our immediate environment. After all, the self and the other always co-exist; anyone that considers only one or the other sees only half of the picture. One extreme falls into subjectivity or solipsism, the other extreme into altruism; both are highly problematic. Now the question is what emotional configuration will sustain both the self and the other in their efforts to cope with their emotions. Regarding emotions, philosophy can guide us by showing the possibilities of such connected intuitive thinking, which relates to our emotional connectivity and 'affectivity' as understood by Spinoza.

Physiological approach

The body and its functions cannot be reduced to mental states and functions, even if we think of forms of thinking that are in tune with bodily functions. Starting with the works of Darwin (1872/1998) and William James, researchers have come to be more concerned about physiological aspects of human emotions. While Hume had focused on the origin of emotions, Darwin explored physical (facial or other) expressions associated with emotions, which we share with animals. For example, what happens to the face and the body in fear, especially in life-threatening situations? Why do we turn red when we are excited, when we feel shame, or when we get very angry? While physiological responses may vary from person to person, they are still there in one form or another. On the other hand, our bodily conditions make us susceptible to specific emotions; for example, if we have disabilities or physical discomforts, we may become irritable and irascible persons and susceptible to such emotions as rage.

Psychological approach

There is much discussion of negative and positive emotions in psychological literature; these terms are used so excessively in psychology that no one understands what they mean any more. In many instances, they are almost arbitrary; for instance, 'anxiety' is considered to be a negative emotion, but Kierkegaard and Heidegger disagree and if psychologists claim to have an intellectual foundation for their thoughts, what would they say? Why do they disagree with Kierkegaard and Heidegger on their conclusion that anxiety is a positive transformation of fear, to use their own term? Instead of positive, 'authentic' would be the proper term. For instance, see Paul McCarthy (Thatcher, Jones, and Lavallee 2014: 168): "Until recently, sport psychologists have known most about negatively toned emotions such as fear and anxiety but much less about positively toned emotions." Later in the same essay, he writes: "negative emotions such as anger, fear, and anxiety create problems in our lives" (171). In some cases, these emotions can contribute to their well-being (McCarthy does talk about happiness in this essay as a core human concern; for instance, when an athlete conquers his or her fear, what we may call anxiety). This type of conquest often gives joy, a sign of strength and powerfulness, to the athlete. One way to approach this discordance regarding the use of emotion-words such as anxiety is to understand the different ways and contexts in which they are used (we have a similar difficulty with the German word 'Mitleid').

Cognitive approach in psychology

'Theories of Emotion Applied to Sport' (e.g. Apter 1989; Lazarus 2000a; Vallerand 1987; Weiner 1986) emphasizes the importance of cognition in the occurrence of emotions. However, it is not universally accepted that all emotions require cognitive processing (see Ekman and Davidson 1994 for a discussion of this issue). Much of this debate centers on how cognition is defined. Using a broad definition of cognition, which includes basic sensory information processing, the elicitation of most, if not all emotions, will involve at least some cognitive processing (Ellsworth 1994). In short, cognition is seen to be central because one does not react in an emotional way to events perceived as meaningless. This cognitive processing may be unconscious and may manifest itself in a physiological response before awareness of the emotion. That a physiological response may precede conscious awareness of an emotional reaction is shown in a study by Bechara, Damasio, Tranei, and Damasio (1997) and Thatcher, Jones, and Lavallee (2014: 40).

Cognition cannot be central to emotion, but only one of its aspects. Emotions do not emerge out of a cognitive process, but are rooted mostly in unconscious psychosomatic functions. Emotions felt can later be analyzed cognitively, but this does not mean that the problematic aspects of emotions can be overcome through such cognitive processing. Unless cognitive theories account for unconscious processes and their primacy, they will remain limited and not sound theories.

An interesting defender of cognitive theory is Robert C. Solomon, although he understands cognition differently. Solomon does not understand cognition simply as knowledge or information, but he seems to consider cognition as a form of overall intelligence. In whatever way he understands cognition, his ideas on emotion are open to debate: his early position was 'we choose our emotions.' As he came to see the loopholes of this position, he later accepted a milder version of his voluntaristic concept of emotion: "there is an enormous range of behaviors and 'undergoings' that might nevertheless be considered within the realm of the voluntary and as matters of responsibility" (2004: 193). To what extent do we really control our emotions or are we in charge of our emotions, especially when we speak of intense emotions, in intense environments like competitive sports in front of thousands of spectators? To what extent is such a theory useful when it comes to explaining those who have issues of anger or jealousy? These emotions are deeply grounded in their psychosomatic being. His defense of his theory is as weak as his dismissal of affective or psychoanalytic theories:

> It suggests a very different kind of framework for the study of emotion, one in which choice, intention, purpose, and responsibility play important, if not central, roles at least some, if not most, of the time. If we think of ourselves as authors of our emotions, we will reflect in such a way as to affect and possibly alter them. It would be nonsense to insist that, regarding our emotional lives, we are 'the masters of our fate,'[11] but nevertheless we are the oarsman, and that is enough to hold that we are responsible for our emotions.
>
> (Solomon 2004: 194)

If we are not the true authors of our emotions, if they originate from our psychosomatic functions that lie deep in our unconscious, then what good is it to believe that we are the authors, especially from the standpoint of overcoming problematic or negative emotions? Sometimes illusions of grandeur can be helpful, but in this case, it is not. It will keep us in our miserable and lower emotional states.

Psychoanalytic approach

Psychoanalysis has been in the forefront in dealing with problems of human emotion because this question was central to Freud. In Freud emotion, feeling, and affect are used almost synonymously due to their affinity; I have already discussed the etymology of these related phenomena elsewhere in this book. So then, let's start with affect. Freud, in an early writing, defines it as "a sum of excitation with which an idea is loaded" (1894: 48). Here the idea, *Vorstellung* in German, refers to a mental image or an idea produced by prior perception of an object, as in memory or imagination, rather than by actual perception. The idea can be attached to other ideas and can produce false connections "it could be dislodged or transposed or could be displaced . . . but essentially it is conceived as a charge seeking for discharge" (Canestri in Fotopoulou, Pfaff and Conway 2014: 179). This is the early Freud who relied on the theory of catharsis, where the ego restricts the resurgence of painful experiences and defense mechanisms are set in place. For instance, in separation anxiety, substitutes are found to replace the objects of love or the love objects of the superego and no deep bonds to others are established so as to prevent a potential separation (such people like my Bohemian friends are always 'on the run'). Accumulated tensions burst into anxiety and other emotions and remain repressed. What remains repressed is explained by Freud in his work 'Repression': Even if the idea remains the same, the affect undergoes vicissitudes of repression which may be different than that which the idea goes through. This quota of affect "corresponds to the instinct in so far as the latter has become detached from the idea and finds expression, proportionate to its quantity [this is what the term 'quota' refers to] in processes which are sensed as affects" (1915: 152). It is interesting that Freud here ties his affect theory to drives – in English translations of Freud's works 'instinct' is also used while Freud rarely uses it in German and sometimes these two terms, 'drive' and 'instinct' are used interchangeably, because they are related; the drive is what drives the basic instinct; more often than not they are hard to separate as much as the animal human is hard to separate from the human animal. "From this point on, in describing a case of repression, we shall have to follow up separately, what, as the result of repression, becomes of the idea, and what becomes of the instinctual energy linked to it" (1915: 152). For example, what happens to the image of the authority figure who abused you and whether or not you still want to kill him or her; of course, all of these remain repressed, what comes out is the expression of its affects in the form of emotions. Following up on the example, an angry hateful person who would want to kill any authority figure or anyone who seems to take on that position. In an interesting twist, Freud says there are no unconscious affects in this same work.

> Strictly speaking, then, and although no fault can be found with the linguistic usage, there are no unconscious affects as there are unconscious ideas. But there may very well be in the system Ucs. affective structures which, like others, become conscious. The whole difference arises from the fact that ideas are cathexes – basically of memory-traces – whilst affects and

feelings correspond to processes of discharge, the final manifestations of which are perceived as sensations. In the present state
of our knowledge of affects and feelings we cannot express this
difference more clearly.

(Freud 1915: 177)

What he seems to be saying, based on his theory of discharge, is that
affects remain to be discharged, whether we understand their cause
and origin or not; in other words, again following up the example,
I was angry when I was abused and am still angry, although I do
not know why I am angry, and in both cases I express my anger in
whatever way or form I find.

However, in his late works, Freud was not satisfied with his discharge theory, namely, that affects or emotions can be understood
simply as functions of discharge. The turn happens in 1926 with
Freud's work 'Inhibitions, Symptoms, and Anxiety' in which anxiety is understood not only as transformation of accumulated tension but also automatic anxiety and anxiety as signal. This new
theory of affect also includes the idea of reminiscence of events and
repetition of experiences, none of which relate directly to discharge,
which seems to be linear while reminiscence or repetition connotes circularity. In this new theory, repetition of previous events
are concocted in different schemes, sometimes even with different
actors, in one's psychic life. I want to add two things rather than
delve further on Freud: first, this new theory corresponds to Freud's
recently acknowledged death drive, 'Thanatos,' which may not be
always interested in discharge. Second, there are emotions that are
not discharge-oriented, such as boredom.

What does all of this psychoanalytic theory mean in a sport context? We all have repressed emotions that we bring along from our
birth – with due respect to psychoanalytical findings, much still
remains in the dark regarding early life emotional experience and
development, because everyone under analysis speaks *ex post facto*
(perhaps child psychoanalysts and psychologists will bring much to
light in this area). These repressed emotions, though always changing, and whether they are traumatic or not, or traumatic in different
degrees, remain repressed if they are not dealt with and complicate
our psychic lives, not to mention our relations with others. Athletes
or members of the sporting community in general are no exceptions
to these psychoanalytic teachings.

Source of emotional problems and possible triggers of negative emotions

Many of our problems stem from repressed emotions, which may stem from in or out of sport contexts. We all have emotional baggage; athletes are not exceptions to this rule. As every approach previously mentioned indicates, what is of utmost importance is to go to the root cause of emotions that are problematic in sport practices. What are those actions that drag athletes, for instance, to rage, despair, grief, and fear? Let's explore those things that may trigger negative emotions in sport practice.

Cheating and unfair practices

Cheating happens in a variety of forms in sport (see Wertz 1981). A common definition of cheating in sport is violation of the rules and standards of a game. They can happen in the field, among players, or originate from external forces outside the field as in game-rigging. Wertz makes several distinctions regarding cheating: detected vs. undetected cheating (1981: 23). If they are never detected by anyone, then they may not create any emotional response. If they are detected by those who are affected by cheating but not by the umpire of the game, such cheats will create anger and resentment among players and their fans. Wertz also makes a distinction between intentional and unintentional forms of cheating (1981: 29–31). Finally, there are forms of self-cheating. One example for such cheating is when bribed athletes, in rigged games for example, underplay or score against their own team so that it is defeated. Whatever the form of cheating is, it destroys the spirit of sport and produces negative emotions and affects that are not conducive to it. I concur with Wertz's reflections on this topic by way of Caillois (2001):

> play is an uncertain activity. The doubt that remains until the end of the game is replaced by the assurance of winning, or something close to it, when cheating occurs. This is incompatible with the nature of play. Not only is its form violated, but also its spirit.
>
> (Wertz 1981: 21)

As Wertz notes later, what he says here applies mostly to competitive sports (I am not suggesting that we should cheat in other sports).

"Cheating attempts to remove the chance element" (1981: 21). But most importantly, cheating is antithetical to the spirit of competing among more or less equals, as it is an attempt to remove fairness and chance from the game.

Intentional or unintentional fouls

Fouls happen all the time in sports and do often produce reactive emotions, especially when there is no tacit agreement for committing them among players in the field and when they go unchecked by umpires. Here I agree with Russell's internalism rather than formalism in sport. Rules can be rewritten by players even if the officialdom falls behind. The other complicated area is whether outright unaccepted fouls are intentional or unintentional. As I was working on this book, the Tour de France (2017) was in progress and Peter Sagan's elbow move that sent Mark Cavendish into a crash with a shoulder and hand injury created much controversy. The investigation is underway, but as of now it is not clear whether Sagan's move was intended to do such harm to his opponent, which disqualified him from the race. Sagan was also disqualified because of his action. These types of actions, whether intentional or not, do provoke much anger and hostility in the sporting community, clearly intentional ones more than unintentional ones. The in-betweens, as in this case, suspend the potential negative emotions. Cavendish had to give a speech to calm his fans.

Under-appreciation

Not esteeming the worth of an athlete can be detrimental for motivation and self-esteem. Properly esteeming and encouraging athletes without necessarily inflating their hubris and arrogance may be a challenge, but is a necessary goal for all trainers and coaches.

Over-expectation

Expecting athletes or teams to do what is almost impossible for them to do could send them into shame or despair. It is hard to control the expectations of fans, but managers and coaches know their teams better than anyone else and need to adjust their expectations accordingly, while always expecting the best from their athletes. Over-ambitious coaches will drive their athletes into the wall.

Emotional shift

Sudden emotional changes may catch athletes and coaches by surprise and unprepared, especially changes from one emotion to its opposite, such as from hope to despair or vice versa. One witnesses such emotional shifts in the rise of underdogs and the fall of overachievers. In such cases, during part of the game hope and dread may alternate, as Jeffrey Fry observes:

> Underdogs are naturally paired with upsets, the second member of our trilogy. Upsets in the making are often emotional roller-coaster rides for participants and fans, who experience alternating hope and dread. At some time during the athletic competition one reaches a turning point when the possibility of an upset becomes believable, or even anticipated. In closely contested games, in which the outcome remains in doubt to the end, the tension is palpable. When underdogs, despite their purported lower position, defy the odds makers by capturing the unexpected victory, they achieve the upset.
>
> (Fry 2017: 17)

In the preceding, I listed some of the sources of emotion, which emerge out of sporting context. Needless to say, athletes have lives outside sporting practices and can have emotional problems related to their background. In addition, problems could arise not exactly in the field or during training, which could create emotional stress, turmoil or trauma in the souls of athletes. One area is the political dimension of sports; the fact that the Russian team was disqualified from the Winter Olympics of 2018 could have created anger and frustration among Russian athletes, even though they could be accepted individually (but a big support in such international games comes from team spirit and fans). Another area is medicine; to give an example from the recent scandal of sexual abuse of USA gymnasts. The abuses by the doctor of the team have created emotional scars in those athletes who were abused. Much of athletic performance depends on athletes' emotional well-being, whether this well-being is achieved in and through sport or not.

What is often forgotten in most of the psychological and psychoanalytic literature, even in Freud, is the question of power. A specific pathos of power, what we can call 'reactive power' by way of Nietzsche and Deleuze, still remains prevalent in our age. Those who are in positions of power prefer not to expose the abuses of their co-powers simply because they too may be subject to scrutiny and lose their position. The fear of loss of power or power position may be connected to self-preservation, shame and/or guilt, which include such issues as honor, prestige, fame, etc. Those who remain silent in cases of abuse of power are also complicit by way of their silence; this should not be forgotten. The problem resides at the roots and has to be addressed from ground up and with an open discussion on how power works and how it connects with our psychosomatic constitutions, including repression. In repressive power relations, the emotional expressions may be silenced; and this creates a major problem for the economy of psychosomatic expenditure and in human well-being and relations.

In conclusion, emotions can be treated, cared for, and healed. Most researchers, philosophers, and psychologists would agree that rage, revenge (in its mediated form), excessive jealousy (the type that leads a lover to kill his/her lover), and excessive guilt (where we always seek someone or something to blame especially when the problem is a shared problem) are emotions that are highly problematic, both for the one who harbors them and for his/her milieu in which they are expressed, in our case, for the sporting community. As Goldie observes, emotions, moods, and character traits are intertwined in the narrative of a person's life (2003: 37); to work on one's emotions also means to work on one's self, to see and accept oneself as always transforming, just like the sporting field. As for healing emotions, one must always contextualize it and understand its origin, object, and circumstance. Such contextualization will help its therapeutic intervention.

Bibliography

Anshel, M. H. (1990). 'Toward Development of a Model for Coping with Acute Stress in Sport'. *International Journal of Sport Psychology* 21, 58–83.

Apter, M. J. (1989). *Reversal Theory: Motivation, Emotion and Personality*. London: Routledge.

Bechara, A. Damasio, H., Tranel D. and Damasio, A. R. (1997). 'Deciding Advantageously Before Knowing the Advantageous Strategy'. *Science* 275, 1293–1295.

Caillois, R. (2001). *Man, Play and Games*. Chicago: University of Illinois Press.

Darwin, C. (1872/1998). *The Expression of the Emotions in Man and Animals*. (ed. by P. Ekman). New York: Oxford University Press.

Delaney, T. (2016). *Sportmanship: Multidisciplinary Perspectives.* Jefferson, NC: McFarland & Company.

Ekman, P. and Davidson, R. J. (1994). *The Nature of Emotion.* Oxford: Oxford University Press.

Ellsworth, P. C. (1994). 'William James and Emotion: A Century of Fame Worth a Century of Misunderstanding?' *Psychological Review* 101:2, 222–229.

Fotopoulou, A., Pfaff, D. and Conway, M. A. (2014). *From the Couch to the Lab: Trends in Psychodynamic Neuroscience.* Oxford: Oxford University Press.

Freud, S. (1894). 'The Neuropsychoses of Defence'. In J. Strachey (ed.), *The Standard Edition of the Complete Psychological Works of Sigmund Freud* (Vol. 3). London: Hogarth Press.

———. (1915). 'Repression'. In J. Strachey (ed.), *The Standard Edition of the Complete Psychological Works of Sigmund Freud* (Vol. 14). London: Hogarth Press.

Fry, J. P. (2017). 'Underdogs, Upsets, and Overachievers'. *Journal of the Philosophy of Sport* 44:1, 15–28.

Goldie, P. (2003). *The Emotions: A Philosophical Exploration.* Oxford: Oxford University Press.

Hume, D. (2000). *A Treatise of Human Nature.* (ed. by D. F. Norton and M. J. Norton). Oxford: Oxford University Press.

Lazarus, R. S. (2000a). 'Cognitive-Motivational-Relational Theory of Emotion'. In Y. L. Hanin (ed.), *Emotions in Sport* (pp. 39–63). Champaign, IL: Human Kinetics.

Solomon, R. (2004). *Thinking about Feeling: Contemporary Philosophers on Emotions* (Series in Affective Science). *What Is an Emotion?: Classic and Contemporary Readings* (2nd Edition). Oxford: Oxford University Press.

Thatcher, J., Jones, M. and Lavallee, D. (2014). *Coping and Emotion in Sport.* London: Routledge.

Vallerand, R. J. (1987). 'Antecedents of Self-Related Affects in Sport: Preliminary Evidence on the Intuitive-Reflective Appraisal Model'. *Journal of Sport Psychology* 9, 161–182.

Weiner, B. (1986). *An Attributional Theory of Motivation and Emotion.* New York: Springer-Verlag.

Wertz, S. K. (1981). 'The Varieties of Cheating'. *Journal of the Philosophy of Sport* 8:1, 19–40.

Chapter 10

Emotion vs. action

Physiological, psychological, linguistic, and rational aspects of emotion

There is a reciprocal interaction between emotions and actions, often creating a vicious circle with negative energies. A player feels anger against an opponent for an undetected foul done to him, keeps the anger within which turns into rage and he uses expletives against this opponent. The opponent, who has almost forgotten the previous foul, does not understand but gets angry. . . . And the cycle continues. Why do we act in this or that way? Why do we get so angry? These questions will remain puzzles; every human being is a unique bundle of emotions, the origins of which remain unknown to him or her for the most part. All of this notwithstanding, we can attempt to seek the origin of emotions in the body, soul, language, and rationality.

Emotion and action

There is a close, reciprocal interaction between emotion and action. First, an action that implicates us, or someone close to us, may provoke a certain kind of emotion. Second, when we are in certain emotional states, especially in intense ones, we can do all sort of things, as in rage, for instance. Not every action entails strong emotions; for example, I am in the library writing these words right now (writing is a form of action) and I have no strong emotions. One would say that I should be joyful that I am doing this work, but that is a general emotion I may have for this book. Right now, at this ninth hour of my library work, I am feeling tired and perhaps even mildly bored. To put it bluntly, today has been a day with no strong emotions for me; at best I could be in a state of 'passive pleasure' to use an Epicurean phrase. I wish someone had made me angry by making noise in this quiet and peaceful space, but that did not happen either.

There is no causal relationship between emotion and action, which applies to all situations. Most people get angry if you harm or slight them. Well, there may be some people who may be indifferent to such things. I am not suggesting that we should harm them in return. Human beings are diverse and experience emotions differently.

As we interact with the world, we feel emotions, which reveal much about ourselves, 'introspective knowledge,' and about other things around us, "extraspective knowledge" (Goldie 2004: 159). Our fears, envies, ambitions, joys, and sufferings bring out much about who we are and how we relate to the world. Goldie goes on to say that both types of feelings can misguide us as much as they reveal to us who we are. We may not be as introspective as these emotions would like to show us; and these emotions may prevent us from understanding others in their authentic selves. "Emotions may be a good thing, but we should not be too optimistic: they come at a certain epistemic cost" (159). The epistemic cost is when we are misguided; our fear may prevent us from knowing who we are and who others are. It can prevent us from a persistent inquiry.

Furthermore, Goldie examines action-emotion relationship, by way of Robert Musil (1996), while keeping in sight the distinction between emotion and mood – associating the former with specify and the latter with non-specificity. Emotions are often directed toward objects, whereas mood is not. Emotions are always dynamic, because they almost always translate themselves into action, which then provokes emotional response, hence creating chains of emotion/action:

> Thus one should not think of an emotion as a disposition which is fixed, with action out of the emotion having no 'feedback' effect on the emotion itself. Emotional experience is, in this sense, more like the unfolding of events in history.
>
> (2004: 6)

Per Goldie, Musil saw this process as one of shaping and consolidating. Whether it is mood or emotion, they are complex human phenomena and are situated within a knot of complex human relations. We often do not know where they come from and where they go.

Athletes must be trained so that they understand the complexity that lies at the root of our emotional experiences and exchanges. Emotions have different intensities and some unworked emotions could be more deeply problematic than others. Someone who has the need to bite his opponent during a game (let's call it "Suarez effect") can easily be channeled to another arena and his problem would be solved, unlike someone else who suffers from rage and may need long-term therapy. We need to distinguish the different intensities of emotional problems at the level of their *affects*.

Sport actions, however, are no ordinary actions, but rather actions of play, that is, 'ludic actions' and play is primordial, as Huizinga shows in *Homo Ludens* (1968), and primarily an activity of joy and pleasure (I do not suggest that sporting field is a field of pleasure only). In his early works, Freud sees play as pleasurable expenditure of psychic energies (1905: 128). If sport is at bottom such a joyful field of action, why then are there all these negative emotions? Now we are going too fast to a conclusion, because Freud, in his later writings, added death drive to his drive theory, which is the source of destruction. If all types of actions, including ludic actions can be said to be driven by Eros and/or Thanatos, then we will have to modify what we said earlier and posit that ludic actions can be joyful and painful, and creative and destructive at the same time. As Holowchak puts it by way of Freud: "the unpleasurable nature of some action does not make it unsuited for play" (2011: 703). On a further note, our main subject in this book is competitive sport; competition also brings about its own economy of emotions and underscores such emotions as ambition and envy, as discussed before, which may not be in all ludic actions per se. Finally, spectators and other members of the sporting community bring their own emotions into the sporting field, hence creating an emotional knot that becomes hard to unravel. Below is yet another attempt to look at emotions in their formation.

Mood vs. emotion: conditions of possibility of feeling emotions

There are conditions that enable human beings to feel emotions. To simplify a complex matter, these conditions can be sought in the processes and functions of the body, the soul, the mind, and language, each of which is an immanent field of multiplicities. The complexity or the non-specificity (using Goldie's qualifier), what we may call 'mood,' lies exactly in the cross-section of these different fields of immanence, which we call 'emotion.' What follows below is an introduction of each of these fields.

Body: instincts, drives, body parts, blood, hormones, organs

Since Charles Darwin, Friedrich Nietzsche, and William James, we have learned to acknowledge the physiological conditions of human emotions. There is reciprocity in this relationship. When we feel a specific emotion, there are physiological changes: muscular reaction, hormonal change, change in facial expression, face turning red, changes in hand gestures, changes in the automatic nervous system, change in the heart beat, sweating, etc. For instance, when we feel fear, the heart starts beating faster. Let's keep in mind that every human being has a different physiological constitution and the physical responses would change from one person to the next. Moreover, a particular response does not mean that I am feeling that emotion associated with that physical condition. If my heart beats faster, it does not mean that I am feeling fear. Lastly, one particular somatic symptom can reflect different emotions, as Miller writes: "if some emotions produce predictable somatic displays, those displays are often susceptible of more than one emotional meaning. . . . Redness can indicate embarrassment, jealousy, anger, indignation, humiliation, or shame" (1995: 103).

On the other hand, somatic conditions often do induce emotional reaction or prepare the ground for it. There are people who have small tolerance for hunger and may be cranky and irascible due to this condition; they would be prone to bursts of anger. There are those who have low tolerance for unusual or disturbing sounds (disturbing to them); this condition is called misophonia. For instance, they could be easily disturbed if someone is eating popcorn next to them in a movie theater. This disturbance creates anger within them, which can explode. There are many other somatic conditions that could adversely impact our emotional being. Physical disabilities could also make people cranky and moody. If the condition is permanent, moodiness may be a chronic part of that person's character. But it must be stated that a causal relationship should not be found here.

As I was working on these manuscripts, I came across yet another amazing book on emotion, *Emotions and the Body*, by Beatrice De Gelder, which examines the connection between bodily expressions (posture, position, shape, etc.) and emotions. As De Gelder (2016) states, most studies in this area have focused on facial expressions (Darwin being one of the pioneers for it) while only few studies looked into the body as a whole. There are, no doubt, historic reasons for this face-centrism, which the author discusses; one being the question as to whether bodily expressions have universal meaning. But more importantly, De Gelder leads the way for presenting research findings and ideas on 'reading' bodily gestures and expressions so as to have some understanding of the emotions of a person (often even before they are expressed).

Soul: images and symbols, dreams, animated parts of the body, etc.

Since we are born or even before, we are bombarded by sense data that are lodged in the depth of our souls. These sense data, in conjunction with our physiological functions, form the basic images and symbols of our being before we speak and way before we become fully cognitive (around 13–15 years old, according to Piaget). Speech and cognition are then superimposed on that constellation, forming a complicated net of disparate, yet somehow connected, elements. Some of these conditions of emotion are transmitted to children from their environment in their pre-linguistic phases.

Freud and psychoanalysis

According to psychoanalysis, much of human life passes with the problems of repression, which stems from renunciation of instincts. Although Freud focuses on the instincts of the libido, Eros, in the early stages of psychoanalysis, he later acknowledges the Death drive and, consequently, the need to fulfill the demands of this drive and its instincts, which means, the need to find proper channels to express aggressivity (sport is one such channel). When the drives of self-preservation do not fully function and the needs are not fulfilled, stemming from the environment and from oneself, then repression occurs; this repression brings about, or is a function of, repressed emotions. The child who is abused cannot express his/her anger and becomes frustrated and this frustration becomes chronic. Or, the child who is misguided in his/her nourishment becomes bitter toward eating and develops eating disorders. These problems in different severities often create such emotions as anger and vengeance, depending on how environmental factors are internalized and whether there are off-setting factors (love and care from someone else, while being abused by parents, for instance). In short, repression creates emotional knots in our souls, tapping into archetypes, as they are embedded in in the registers of the Real, the Symbolic, and the Imagery (using Lacan's terminology). And it may take a lifetime to unravel these knots, because that would entail dissolving bonds (sometimes even relationships) and reconstructing new bonds, all of which can be a painful process. There is, in human life, a tendency to sustain the status-quo, because no one can be certain of the outcome when things become topsy-turvy.

Athletes are not exceptions to the rules of psychic phenomena and suffer from their own forms of repression, formed by their own upbringing, formation, and environment. What interests me is to understand how the sporting field, which is rife with emotional experiences like love relations, can be a space for psychoanalytic intervention especially for the therapy of problem-emotions such as rage, excessive guilt, fear, and (unprocessed) anxiety. Many common emotional problems in sport, such as outbursts of anger, performance anxiety, despair, hubris, and blaming others (especially when blame is to be shared), are some general areas for such intervention.

Language: words and speech, names, propositions; semantics vs. syntax

Language is a system of signs unlike other signs, which consists of semantic and syntactic fields. Every language has its own semantic field, and every language family has its own syntactic properties. But how does emotion relate to language? One very old theory is that of Stoics, which construes emotions as judgments. For Nietzsche, on the other hand, language is never an adequate form of expression (in contrast to music, for instance) and there is no direct correspondence between words and feelings. Language can never fully reflect our emotions and emotional state of being. Wittgenstein considered language a game; we know what emotion-word to use in this game. Finally, Saussure conceived of language to be an immanent system of signification; we know the difference between envy and jealousy because of their difference in sound and what they signify. Although emotion-words enable us to analyze, evaluate, and understand our emotional states, they cannot cover the entire emotive field and also can misguide us regarding our emotional states. As Miller rightly observes: "They [emotion-words] tend to make us subsume our emotional states . . . into the ready-made category the word provides. Emotion terms, like all words, generalize and in the process fuzz over a lot of individual variation" (1995: 101).

Mind: thinking, abstract in its pure form; intuitive when connected to emotions and feelings

Abstract thinking is conceptual thinking that forms ideas, establishes connections, and helps formulate different types of propositions. From the standpoint of abstract thinking, emotions are just mental states expressed in emotion-words and propositions, and can be understood fully, in cognitive terms, and controlled. This form of thinking disregards psychosomatic functions or subordinates it to a lesser level and treats emotions as though they are fully transparent and understandable. On the other hand, it does not consider any fusion, such as emotional forms of thinking. Intuitive thinking (similar to introspection) is a form of thinking that is in touch with internal states, including emotions and feelings. It does not negate the role of emotions; on the other hand, it reflects on emotions and learns something from it and creates a fusion. Concomitantly, it sees an emotional dimension in thought. An intuitive person who feels anger, for instance, would ask why he/she feels it while being connected within and without, whereas the rationalist type, in line with abstract thinking, will be defensive about his/her anger, no matter what, and analyze it to an end (rationalists put up logically knit defense mechanisms rather than be introspective about who they are).

Time and emotion

Some scholars claim that emotions are transient and they make a distinction between what is transient and what is more permanent in our sentimental being. Jones and Uphill contrast emotion to mood in terms of their relationship to duration, magnitude, and object (Thatcher, Jones and Lavallee 2014: 34); our concern here is its relationship to time. Whether transient or not, we need to keep examining the conditions of possibility of emotions and here we cannot ignore conceptions of time, in addition to the conditions listed previously. Although emotions may be transient, there are enduring conditions that reside in our being, which enable us to feel such and such an emotion in a specific context. We can tentatively say that all these 'a priori' conditions are to be found in 'mood' including temporality.

Although time is one of those complicated subjects in philosophy, we can simplify all time conceptions into two types: linear/

progressive vs. cyclical. The first one construes time as a chain of events that happen one after another, a unidirectional flow of all happenings; this has stamped the time experience of Occidental civilization since ancient Greeks (the best representatives for this model are Aristotle and modern science). The cyclical conception, on the other hand, conceives time as repetition, repetition of cycles of creation and destruction, in which all times blend together and life and death are conjoined; here we can count all ancient societies, including the Pre-Socratic and Homeric one, Hinduism, Buddhism (the idea of karma), and St. Augustine, and, from recent times, Nietzsche, Bergson, and Heidegger. Now, how does time, or these different paradigms, relate to emotion and mood?

There are emotions that are clearly stamped by time signature such as mediated revenge, boredom, and anger. In revenge, I ruminate over a harm done to me and make plans to get back at the one who harmed me. I cannot bury that single event into eternity and forget it, but rather become fixated on it. Similarly, in boredom one feels the pain of linear time, because linear time as focused on real events leaves not much room in terms of fantasy and dream. Today's gadgets deprive children from the richness of a mythic, fantastic world and they get bored easily in this world of linear time.

The sporting world is not free from the signature of this linear time, which also makes sport teleological (goal-oriented) in our age, whereas sport is playful, process-oriented, and ultimately not telic. The end is only a temporary end; what counts is the process of playing. Ancient athletes, specifically Olympic and Panhellenic athletes of ancient Greece, did not play under the pressure of time; the goal set, such as winning a race, was only a temporary stop in the eternal play of time. In combat games athletes played until the very end, until one of them gave up (if not died already). Similarly, some of the emotions felt carry the signature of linear time, including such emotions as blame and guilt. Archaic societies knew shame, in which human actions and emotions were supposed to be in tune with higher orders (cyclical), whereas we suffer from guilt, which is supposed to be dealt with punishment later in time (linear). The main punishment in today's world, prison term, is also a function of linear time.

Space and context

Every emotion emerges in a specific context in which its object is presented. In sport, that can be the field of sport, training, or an actual game, with or without spectators or umpires. Space provides the unique constellation for all members of the sporting community, called a 'game,' in which emotions are expressed. In the total emotional experience of a game, we must count all the expressions; however, the players, especially star players, due to the extent of their influence, coaches due to their position of power, and the intensity of emotions seem to play more of a determinant role in the total outcome. It must also be noted that intensive negative emotions often provoke reactions and create more of an impact. Architects design the space, builders build it, and organizers place the players, umpires, and spectators in the constellation of the game. Spatially and contextually, much has been already determined and much falls on the shoulders of organizers to sustain the spirit of sporting. If one puts an athlete who is provocative next to or on the opposing side of an athlete who is explosive, there will be explosion just like fire and gas together.

Inner vs. outer

One thing that has troubled scholars who worked on the question of feelings and emotions is the fact that they are, to a large extent, internal phenomena. We experience others' emotions only when they are felt and expressed in some form or another (not only linguistically, of course). Now the question is: what is the bridge that links the internal world to the external one? One notion in this area can shed light on the problem, and that is the notion of "psychic feeling" (Stocker 1983: 25), which has to do with care, concern, and interest. In other words, our emotional constitution has much to do with our disposition toward life, or our being-in-the-world, and our being-with-others, which are rooted in and can be explained in terms of these three functions. Before we even feel emotions, we are already under the rules of care, concern, and interest. This idea, no doubt, throws a different ontological wrench to the problem of emotion, because, so far in this book, we have focused on the primary registers of human emotions such as body, soul, mind, and language. Now, how do care, concern, and interest fit into the picture? At the outset, we can say that these three are relational; they have to do with our connection to the world and functions of our relationship to the world and what moves these three are the affectations, that is, the motions or excitations of affects at primordial registers, what are often called 'desire.' For instance, why some people lack motivation must be sought in this area of psychic feelings, before we can even examine why and how they feel such and such emotion.

In conclusion of this chapter, let it suffice to say that there is a congruity, a correlation, if not a casual relationship, between emotion and action. There are also conditions of possibility of feeling emotions; I adduced six areas for these conditions, as shown previously, each of which needs to be studied in its own right. One does not feel emotions in void, but rather due to these psychosomatic, mental, linguistic, temporal, and spatial conditions that are both given and yet appropriated by individuals.

Epilogue for Part III

Emotional well-being, performance, sportsmanship, and the spirit of sport

Every type of sport is unique and demands its own sets of skills; so is the athlete with his/her unique emotional being. There is a set of emotions, often uplifting, high-energy emotions, that enable athletes to function at their highest capacity. This is applicable to the general mood of athletes and their disposition to the competition as they enter it, for instance, their ability to handle their fear and anxiety. Although this subject was addressed previously, there is another context for anxiety in which it is presented, often in psychological literature, in its debilitative effect. Here anxiety can prevent athletes from fulfilling their better performance. Furthermore, there are emotions that enable them to play well such as ambition to win and pride in one's success, but also to play well together such as controlled anger and ambition, and moderated, self-reflective blame. Lastly, there are emotions that are in congruence with the sporting tasks at hand. For instance, high levels of arousal as one finds in anxiety, anger, and excitement, can increase anaerobic power and, therefore, can be good for jumping. On the other hand, increased arousal may not be good for tasks that require fine motor control, balancing, and concentration as in weightlifting, golf, and archery (Thatcher, Jones, and Lavallee 2014: 43–48).

Bibliography

De Gelder, B. (2016). *Emotions and the Body*. New York: Oxford University Press.

Freud, S. (1905). 'Jokes and Their Relation to the Unconscious'. In J. Strachey (ed. & trans.), *Standard Edition of the Complete Psychological Works of Sigmund Freud* (Vol. 18). London: Hogarth Press.

Goldie, P. (2004). 'Emotion, Feeling and Knowledge of the World'. In R. Solomon (ed.), *Thinking about Feeling* (pp. 91–106). New York: Oxford University Press.

Holowchak, M. A. (2011). 'Freud on Play, Games, and Sports Fanaticism'. *Journal of the American Academy of Psychoanalysis and Dynamic Psychiatry* 39:4, 695–716.

Huizinga, J. (1968). *Homo Ludens: A Study of the Play Element in Culture*. Boston: Beacon Press.

Miller, W. I. (1995). *Humiliation: And Other Essays on Honor, Social Discomfort, and Violence*. Ithica: Cornell University Press.

Musil, R. (1996). *The Man without Qualities*. (transl. by S. Wilkins and B. Pike). New York: Vintage.

Stocker, M. (1983). 'Psychic Feelings: Their Importance and Irreducibility'. *Australasian Journal of Philosophy* 61, 5–26.

Thatcher, J., Jones, M. and Lavallee, D. (2014). *Coping and Emotion in Sport*. London: Routledge.

Epilogue

One of the main inspirational ideas for embarking on this project was to understand the emotional aspect of the spirit of sport. I uphold that the spirit of sport exists in an uncanny balance of 'appropriate' emotions; that is to say, athletes must harbor and express the 'appropriate' emotions, at the right time and to the right degree. They must be ambitious to compete, but their ambition should not exceed the context of their specific game. If defeated, athletes must accept their defeat and learn from it; if victorious, they must handle their victory with caution. Ambition for that game ends when the game ends. The victorious, of course, must celebrate their victory, but not ostentatiously, which could strip the opponent of their dignity and make them feel shame; the pain of humiliation for the defeated is sufficient. On the other hand, we may get angry when our teammates make mistakes, but that anger should not persist for too long, because it will not benefit the one who feels it, nor will it benefit one's teammates. The constructive impact of blame has a limit. To learn from our mistakes together is more constructive/ positive. While the examples of appropriate emotions are manifold, one may wonder how, if subjective, they can be 'appropriate.' Although emotions are generally considered purely subjective, that is contentious. Emotions are fostered collectively, with some being permitted expression while others are not, as they evolve in our 'affective' power relations.

On the other hand, one must exercise caution in making gross generalizations about human emotions, which philosophers from Plato to Adam Smith have done – open almost any book of that span of time and you will encounter many general remarks about the human condition and emotion; however, they do not apply to every single case. Human beings are diverse and their emotional constitution stems from both their own individual selves and environment and the interaction of the two; such an emotional constitution differs from culture to culture as well and can be informed by one's religious background. Lastly, every human being is a unique configuration of emotions. This point does not negate what I said previously regarding the spirit of sport and the necessity for 'appropriate' emotions for the spirit of sport. To reconcile the two points, I would say that athletes, who have their own unique emotional constitutions, must attune such constitutions to the spirit of sport through their 'sentimental education'; if they don't, they could not be deemed to be 'good athletes.'

The sporting field harbors complex, sometimes opposing, emotions. Within the same community, there are athletes who celebrate their victory in a state of euphoria and those who experience their defeat as a state of grief. The presence of complex emotions within the same space often creates confusion and confused behavior; while one athlete is joyful for the victory of his or her team, their opponent may be in a state of sadness for the defeat of his or hers.

Furthermore, we must be cognizant of the affects our emotional responses may create, especially if we are in touch with our emotions. The sporting community must be sensitive to the emotional needs and maturity of its members, including both athletes and spectators alike. It is in the spirit of emotional attunement that I dedicated my time and labor to this philosophical endeavor.

As Barbara Keys states, "understanding the role of emotion is critical if we are to grasp the full dimensions of human behavior" (2013: 29). While every human being is a unique configuration of emotions, we have neglected the study, and more importantly, the care, of emotions for so long, suffering from the hegemony of the intellect, its reactive impact on all that is not itself, not to mention other socio-cultural problems. "We have perhaps forgotten to pay sufficient attention to the most basic sources of sport's power and influence" (2013: 33). It is time to reverse this trend and to examine the deep passions and emotions that lie at the root of sporting culture with the hope that members of the sporting community from athletes to umpires, coaches, and fans do the same. In this way, we can try to undo the impact of 'negative' emotions to some extent, those emotions that stem either from the sporting field or from society at large. I do not suggest that we get rid of negative emotions entirely or desire to do so as in A Clockwork Orange. On the contrary, in this book I have argued for the refinement and sublimation of negative emotions that are destructive to human beings and disruptive to the spirit of sport and for the creation of positive affects in the public arena. It would be too idealistic to suggest that we can eliminate our negative emotions.

Many psychologists of sport argue that 'mental toughness' (Mellalieu and Hanton 2009: 322) is an integral element for achieving success in sport, which includes physical well-being, skill, and experience (Luszki 1982), or self-discipline, self-sacrifice, and teamwork (Tunney 1987). Mental toughness, however, cannot be equated (or confused) with emotional toughness, or what I call 'emotional maturity.' In fact, as typically used, 'mental toughness' almost always connotes emotional toughness (or hardness/calcification), which is highly problematic. While I agree with their list, while not dismissing mental toughness, I would add 'emotional maturity' to the components necessary for being a good/great athlete.

Emotions and the related phenomena such as affects, sentiments, moods, and feelings play a variety of roles in human life. First, they emanate signs for others to receive, interpret, and respond to (I am speaking of emotions expressed in public arenas, as in sporting contexts). Coaches and trainers have to be astute interpreters of emotional signs so as to be able to determine when their athletes are emotionally distressed in a given situation, especially when on the field competing. Second, emotions reveal one element of who we are as persons, including our character strengths and weaknesses. Third, negative emotions show what must be overcome and transformed. This is not to say that we can eliminate negative emotions entirely, but we can work on them and elevate some of them to their higher forms; each emotion needs its own care, as I had proposed earlier. On the other hand, and not to contradict what I have been arguing for, negative emotions do serve their own functions. Fear can save your life, but excessive fear would paralyze you and prevent you from acting. Fourth, emotions indicate what action to take in specific situations; for instance, our fear can help alert us to wild, hungry animals and therefore serve to protect us. Finally, emotions help us to regulate our actions and behaviors in relation to ourselves and others.

There is no single recipe or theory of emotion that could apply to every situation. Human beings are distinct configurations of unique emotions. However, we can adapt existing ideas and theories, which are appropriate to a holistic conception of the spirit of sport, and in this way develop them so that they help heal our emotional problems. There are times when an emotion needs to be discharged. When there are emotional problems, we need to be introspective and investigate the origin and quality of those emotions; although we feel emotions, they occur in the rudimentary registers of the human soul and body, as they produce and disseminate various affects; these affects take their place in lateral and vertical power relations. This theoretical framework, which I use in this book, covers a substantial territory, but it is far from complete. Also, there are instances when it is best to withdraw from a conflict with intense emotions, where remaining in such a conflict would only bring more harm and produce more negative affects. In such cases, it may be best to follow the Stoic and Taoist approaches of 'apathia' and 'wu wei wu'; the former teaches us to be detached our immediate circumstances and the latter promotes the idea of 'no action.' Even if detachment may not be the best thing to do for a situation (especially from the standpoint of emotional therapy), remaining in the conflict will not help us manage the emotional problem insofar as we are implicated in that problem. Sometimes we are deadlocked in conflicts and the emotional problems they perpetuate; this happens because we are unable to withdraw from the conflict for different reasons. If we learn how to withdraw, we can at least prevent the problematic emotion to be fed with its object all the time. Having deprived the object of that emotion, what remains to do is to go to the root of that emotion.

Finally, human beings, including athletes and other members of the sporting community, are distinct configurations of unique emotions. In unusual circumstances, as in competitive sports when the stakes are high and when the games are 'dangerous,' intense emotions will always be felt and expressed, often without any reserve. Hence, we cannot escape our emotional composition. However, we can be introspective about our emotions and be sensitive to the kinds of affects they may produce and be more mindful of the effect they can have upon others.

Bibliography

Keys, B. (2013). 'Senses and Emotions in the History of Sport'. *Journal of Sport History* 40:1, 21–38.

Luszki, W. A. (1982). *Winning Tennis through Mental Toughness*. New York: Everest House.

Mellalieu, S. D. and Hanton, S. (2009). *Advances in Applied Sport Psychology*. New York: Routledge.

Tunney, J. (1987). 'Thoughts on the Line. Mental Toughness: Biceps for the Mind'. *Soccer Journal* 32, 49–50.

Index